Women Win the Vote

The Hard-Fought Battle for Women's Suffrage

Larry A. Van Meter

 Enslow Publishers, Inc.
40 Industrial Road
Box 398
Berkeley Heights, NJ 07922
USA
http://www.enslow.com

America's
Living History

Library of Congress Cataloging-in-Publication Data:

Van Meter, Larry A.
Women win the vote : the hard-fought battle for women's suffrage / Larry A. Van Meter.
   p. cm.
Includes bibliographical references and index.
Summary: "Discusses the history of the women's suffrage movement in the United States, including the origins of the movement, the key figures in the struggle for suffrage, and the Nineteenth Amendment granting women the right to vote"—Provided by publisher.
   ISBN-13: 978-0-7660-2940-8
   ISBN-10: 0-7660-2940-9
   1. Women—Suffrage—United States—History—Juvenile literature. 2. Suffragists—United States—History—Juvenile literature. I. Title.
   JK1898.M48 2009
   324.6'230973—dc22

                              2008024900

Printed in the United States of America

10 9 8 7 6 5 4 3 2 1

♻ Enslow Publishers, Inc., is committed to printing our books on recycled paper. The paper in every book contains 10% to 30% post-consumer waste (PCW). The cover board on the outside of each book contains 100% PCW. Our goal is to do our part to help young people and the environment too!

To Our Readers: We have done our best to make sure all Internet Addresses in this book were active and appropriate when we went to press. However, the author and the publisher have no control over and assume no liability for the material available on those Internet sites or on other Web sites they may link to. Any comments or suggestions can be sent by e-mail to comments@enslow.com or to the address on the back cover.

Illustration Credits: Archives and Special Collections, Mount Holyoke College, p. 40; Associated Press, p. 112; Courtesy Special Collections, University of Virginia Library, p. 35; Denver Public Library #F12978, p. 92; Enslow Publishers, Inc., pp. 58, 105; The Granger Collection, New York, pp. 21, 37, 60, 85; J. Paul Getty Museum #84.XT.1582.5, p. 64; Library and Archives Canada / C-029977, p. 90; Library of Congress, pp. 9, 15, 31, 47, 50, 74, 78, 94, 98, 102, 108, 110; National Archives and Records Administration, p. 82; National Woman's Party, p. 104; Oberlin College, p. 39; Special Collections Vassar College, p. 70; © Visual Arts Library (London) / Alamy, p. 26.

Illustration Used in Running Heads: Library of Congress (sculpture).

Cover Illustration: Shutterstock Images © Lisa F. Young (Young first-time voter, foreground); Library of Congress (Suffragette, background).

Contents

Chapter 1

Victory in Wyoming

Be it enacted by the Council and House of Representatives of the Territory of Wyoming:

Sec. 1. That every woman of the age of twenty-one years, residing in this Territory, may at every election to be holden under the law thereof, cast her vote. And her rights to the elective franchise and to hold office shall be the same under the election laws of the territory, and those of electors.

—From a December 10, 1869 Wyoming law granting women in that territory the right to vote.

In 1869, American women did not have the right to vote. They would not gain that right for more than half a century. But 1869 would prove to be important in the struggle for women's voting rights. That year, in Washington D.C., the nation's capital, a new constitutional amendment, the Fifteenth Amendment, was being introduced to grant suffrage, or the right to vote, to African-American men. It was an important step in overcoming the racism that had marked American history. And women's rights activists were hoping to add women's suffrage to the new law.

Meanwhile, in the Wyoming Territory, events were unfolding that would be significant in the American women's suffrage movement. At the center of those events in Wyoming was Esther Morris, a saloon owner in South Pass City, one of the largest towns in the territory.

In 1869, there were thirty-seven states in the United States. As was true for many areas in the American West, Wyoming was a "territory," a geographic area that did not yet have statehood status. Like many people in Wyoming, Morris wanted Wyoming to become a state. She had been working with many others to organize a legislature for the Wyoming Territory. The Wyoming territorial elections were to take place on September 3, 1869. Those elections were going to be a very important step in Wyoming's bid to become a new state.

The United States was quickly growing. The nation had recently reunified after the Civil War had ended in 1865. Statehood was the goal of all territories. It meant full partnership in this vast, new country—a country still less than a century old. Gaining statehood, however, was difficult. The territories had to prove themselves worthy of entry into the union. And what did Wyoming, the least populated of all the territories, have to offer? In 1869, the population of Wyoming was a meager 8,014[1], too small to be considered for statehood. The requirement for statehood was a population of over 25,000.

Esther Morris had a plan to gain the attention of the lawmakers in the nation's capital. Her plan would surely put Wyoming on the map of the United States.

Beginnings

Born in Oswego, New York, in 1814, Esther McQuigg Morris grew up in an orphanage. Trained to be a seamstress as a young girl, she was hardworking and—unlike many women in the nineteenth century—financially successful. At the age of twenty-eight, she married Artemus Slack, a civil engineer. In 1842, they had a son, Archibald. Tragedy struck in 1845 when Artemus died. Esther then moved with Archibald from New York to Illinois to settle Slack's financial affairs. At that time, however, women had few legal rights. Legally, a woman was considered chattel, that is, her husband's property. If the husband died before his wife, she faced a difficult legal battle to gain the family property and money. Esther was unable to secure the Illinois property that her husband had left to her. The harsh legal battles regarding Slack's property left Esther frustrated, making her sensitive to women's rights.[2]

Those legal hardships would play a strong role in forming Esther's resolve. While in Illinois, she married a local merchant, John Morris. After the birth of twins, Robert and Edward, the Morrises, like thousands of Americans at the time, went west to seek their fortune.

In 1868, they moved to South Pass City in the Wyoming Territory, one of the many gold mining towns that were sprouting in the American West.

The Morrises opened a saloon, a successful business that established the couple as influential, well-respected citizens. And like many citizens on the American frontier, the couple wanted statehood for Wyoming.

Esther Morris Has a Great Idea

In the same way that states established their own legislatures—a governing body that makes laws—the territories also organized legislatures. But a territorial legislature was not only a lawmaking body, it was also required for statehood. If a territory could run a government, it would prove that it could handle the responsibility of statehood. Two candidates for the territorial legislature, William H. Bright and Herman G. Nickerson, were in South Pass City for the elections. Bright was the Democratic Party candidate for the legislature, and Nickerson was a Republican candidate. Both Bright and Nickerson were veterans of the Civil War, and both were acquaintances of Esther Morris. They both held Morris in high regard. Because Morris was one of the most prominent citizens in South Pass City, Bright and Nickerson knew that gaining her approval would help to secure election to the legislative office.

Esther Morris was respected by men and women alike in the Wyoming Territory.

Almost six feet tall, Morris was admired for her fairness, honesty, and confidence. She commanded respect from everyone she met. Morris realized that the best strategy to earn statehood for Wyoming was to bring thousands of people to live there. Her idea to get them there was to give women the right to vote. As the elections neared, Morris approached Bright and Nickerson with her idea. At first they were stunned. At that time, no women had the right to vote anywhere in the world! The two candidates eyed her suspiciously— was she serious? Both men quickly recognized the importance of Morris's suggestion. This bold move would indeed draw the attention of the American people. Even those people who had never heard of the Wyoming Territory would take notice if Wyoming was considering women's suffrage. Perhaps when people learned about Wyoming, they would want to move there.

Bright was the first to promise Morris that, if elected to the legislature, he would introduce a women's suffrage bill. Not wanting to be outdone by his opponent, Nickerson also promised that he would introduce such a bill if elected. Word spread rapidly through town that something big was planned for the new territorial legislature.

Bright won the election. Would he be true to his word? It was one thing to promise suffrage to a woman before the elections, but quite another to introduce a women's suffrage bill in the legislature. The first Wyoming territorial legislature convened in Cheyenne on October 1, 1869. All eyes were on the new senator. If Bright was nervous about the attention, he was not letting on. So cool and confident did he appear, as a matter of fact, that he was elected president of the nine-man Senate.

Esther Morris's Idea Blossoms

On November 9, William H. Bright announced during a Senate session that in a few days he was going to make a major proposal. Sure enough, on November 12, he stood up and announced his bill: "An act to Grant the Women of Wyoming Territory the Right of Suffrage and to Hold Office." There were a few laughs and insults thrown at Bright, but the senators had known in advance that the bill was coming.

After the announcement, Bright had two weeks to convince his fellow senators to vote *for* the bill. It should be noted that none of the other senators were for the bill. The senators did not really believe that women should have the right to vote. But they did understand that the bill was a big deal. It was front-page news all over the Wyoming Territory, and it was drawing the attention of the East Coast newspapers as well. Bright tried to convince the senators that, whether or not they actually agreed with the bill, passage of the bill would be a dramatic and symbolic statement for the Wyoming Territory. Furthermore, passage of the bill could draw homesteaders out to the new territory. After all, Wyoming needed several thousand more citizens to qualify for statehood.

Working with Esther Morris and his wife, Julia, Bright managed to be very persuasive. The suffrage bill passed by a 6-2 margin. (One senator was absent.) This was the first time in history that a women's suffrage bill had passed in a legislative body. But Bright's "Female Suffrage Act," as it would become known in the territory, was only one-third of the way to becoming law. After its passage in the territorial Senate, it would go to the territorial House of Representatives for approval. If it was approved there, the territorial governor, John Campbell, would then have to approve and sign it.

Esther Morris and Julia Bright, thrilled by the bill's success passing that first test, began a letter-writing campaign to the territorial representatives, urging them to pass the women's suffrage bill. Even more important, the two major newspapers in Cheyenne endorsed the bill. The *Wyoming Tribune*, for example, announced that the bill "is likely to be THE measure of the session, and we are glad our Legislature has taken the initiative in this movement, which [is] destined to become universal.

Better to appear to lead than hinder when a movement is inevitable."[3]

Despite the letter-writing and the favorable treatment in the newspapers, there was heated debate on the bill. As in the Senate, there was opposition to the bill in the House. One representative, Ben Sheeks, joked that the minimum age in the bill (eighteen) should be changed to thirty, on the theory that no woman would admit to being thirty years old. This type of humor was typical for men then. They were convinced that women were not serious about getting involved in American government. Many men—and women as well—believed that women were too emotional and too weak to have a say in politics. Many people feared that women's suffrage would disturb the traditional household arrangements, where husbands and fathers dominated. But after the debates, the eleven-member House voted on the bill. By the narrowest of margins, the House passed the bill: six votes for, four against, with one abstention. The only hurdle remaining was Governor Campbell.

However, very few people actually believed that the "Female Suffrage Act" would become Wyoming law. Perhaps the biggest problem concerned politics: Most of the senators and representatives in Wyoming were members of the Democratic Party. But Governor Campbell was a Republican who constantly found himself at odds with the legislature. That rivalry was one of the reasons that many of the legislators had passed the bill. They fully expected Campbell to veto—a legal term meaning "to reject"—the women's suffrage bill. In other words, the legislators promised William Bright that they would vote for the bill, but they never expected it to become law. They believed that their political rival, Governor Campbell, would never sign it. It was public knowledge that Campbell did not like the bill, having said on several occasions that he did not support women's suffrage. And if he were to veto the bill, then its only chance of becoming law would be for the legislature to override his veto. The legislature needed a two-thirds majority to override a governor's veto—and the Wyoming legislators knew no such majority existed. If Campbell vetoed the bill, it would "die," meaning that it would not become law.

But by the time the women's suffrage bill landed on his desk, Governor Campbell had experienced a change of heart. He had noticed the impassioned defense of the bill by some men and women in the territory and the favorable treatment of the bill in the state newspapers. Governor Campbell believed that the bill was a good thing after all. He understood that passage of the women's suffrage bill would not only be an important moment in Wyoming history but also in American history. So on December 10, 1869, John Campbell, governor of the Wyoming Territory, signed the women's suffrage bill into law.

WOMAN SUFFRAGE IN WYOMING TERRITORY.—SCENE AT THE POLLS IN CHEYENNE.
FROM A PHOTO. BY KIRKLAND.—SEE PAGE 221.

This illustration from *Frank Leslie's Illustrated Newspaper* shows women voting in Cheyenne in Wyoming Territory on November 24, 1888.

Esther Morris Helps Ignite a Movement

For the first time, women had the right to vote. Of course, that right was limited to women in the Wyoming Territory, and there was no guarantee that Wyoming would keep women's suffrage if it became a state. Nevertheless, for at least as long as Wyoming was a territory, women had the right to vote. Behind the new law was Esther Morris, who had risen from an orphanage to become one of the most important people in the women's suffrage movement.

But Morris's work as a feminist pioneer was not over. Just a few months after women's suffrage was legalized in Wyoming, Morris became a judge in South Pass City. She was the first woman to hold a judicial position.[4] On February 17, 1870, Morris was granted a commission to serve as justice of the peace for South Pass City, a position she held for eight months. After she left the position, the *South Pass News* ran a story on Morris, saying, "Mrs. Justice Esther Morris retires from her judicial duties today. She has filled the position with great credit to herself and secured the good opinion of all with whom she has transacted any official business."[5]

Wyoming gained statehood in 1890, becoming the forty-fourth state in the Union. To the delight of women's suffrage activists all over America, Wyoming elected to keep women's suffrage when it became an official state. Statehood was celebrated in Cheyenne, the capital city, on July 24, 1890.

The honor of presenting the new state flag to the governor fell to Morris, then in her seventies, who said:

> On behalf of the women of Wyoming, and in grateful recognition of the high privilege of citizenship that has been conferred upon us, I have the honor to present to the state of Wyoming this beautiful flag. May it always remain the emblem of our liberties, "and the flag of the union forever."[6]

To present the newest flag in the United States to the governor was a great honor, but it was also a fitting tribute to Esther Morris, who, after all, had been one of the pioneers in the women's suffrage movement.

Chapter $\boxed{2}$

A New Country

The struggle to gain women's suffrage—the right for women to vote—in the United States had raged for several decades before 1869, the year of Wyoming's famous suffrage bill. By then, high-profile women's suffrage activists, such as Elizabeth Cady Stanton, Susan B. Anthony, and Lucy Stone, had become household names in America. But they had not achieved voting rights for women. Though voting was now legal for women in the Wyoming Territory, women were denied that right everywhere else in the United States— in fact, no women anywhere else in the world had the right to vote, either.

Still, the fight for women's suffrage had come a long way. The seeds of women's suffrage had been planted almost a century before the success in Wyoming.

Suffrage in the Early United States

The year 1789 was an important year in world history. Then, two countries an ocean apart, the United States and France, would play roles in the drama of women's suffrage. Two other dates in American history are more famous—1776 (the signing of the Declaration of Independence) and 1787 (the drafting of the U.S. Constitution). But 1789 is noteworthy because that year the new United States ratified its Constitution, the document that defined the American government.

Between the years 1776 and 1789, a debate about voting rights raged among the founding fathers of the United States. All of them agreed that the right to vote was very important. Many called it the "First Liberty." But the debate was not over whether one should have the right to vote, but rather over *who* should have the right to vote. In the Declaration of Independence, Thomas Jefferson wrote these profound words: "We hold these truths to be self-evident: that all men are created equal." Those were bold and revolutionary words, implying that *all* men—regardless of where they were born or who their parents were—should have the chance at freedom and liberty. Though these were true and hopeful words in 1776, they excluded more than half the American population. Women were not considered equal, and they certainly were not considered when the founding fathers were debating the issue of suffrage. Many of the founding fathers were wealthy landowners who thought that only those who owned property should be granted suffrage.

"Remember the Ladies"

Thomas Jefferson gave John Adams, a lawyer from Massachusetts, the nickname "Colossus of Independence." Just like Jefferson and Benjamin Franklin, Adams was an original member of the Continental Congress. As the Continental Congress met in the summer of 1776 to declare the colonies independent from England, Adams and his colleagues understood that they were building a new country. Though they were all united in their desire to build a country free from tyranny and injustice, many were unsure about how they should organize this new country. Who would be the leaders? Who would have the right to choose those leaders?

Adams, whose family owned a large farm in eastern Massachusetts, believed that only male property owners should have the right to vote. Indeed, that restriction was the law in all the colonies at the time of the Declaration of Independence. But should it remain the law when the new country broke away from England? Several men in the Continental Congress were calling for an expansion of voting rights to men who did not own property. Adams was shocked at this suggestion, saying:

> [I]t is dangerous to open up so fruitful a source of
> controversy and altercation as would be opened by

attempting to alter the qualifications of voters; there will be no end of it. New claims will rise; women will demand a vote; lads from twelve to twenty-one will think their rights not enough attended to; and every man who has not a farthing will demand an equal voice.[1]

To Adams and many other men, "universal suffrage" (a term meaning that any adult could vote) was a frightening idea. Adams wanted the new American government—a democracy—to be different from the monarchy in England. However, he wanted the suffrage rules to be similar to those in England, where property ownership was the chief requirement for the right to vote.

But one person who did not agree with Adams lived under his own roof—his wife, Abigail! She was afraid that the Continental Congress was

Gilbert Stuart painted this portrait of Abigail Adams sometime between 1800 and 1815, while the former first lady was still alive.

ignoring too many people's voices, particularly women's voices. In March 1776, she wrote a letter to her husband: "I long to hear you have declared an independency, and, by the way, in the new code of laws which I suppose it will be necessary for you to make, I desire you would remember the ladies, and be more generous and favorable to them than your ancestors. Do not put such unlimited power into the hands of husbands."[2]

Later in the same letter, Abigail warned her husband that if he did not include women in the new government, they would "foment a rebellion." These were bold words, especially for the wife of a prominent member of the Continental Congress. John Adams wrote back to his wife: "The Declaration's wording specifies that 'all *men* are created equal.'"

Abigail's words—"Remember the ladies"—would become a famous rallying cry for women's suffrage, but her husband ignored them.

Thomas Paine Makes His Case

Another person who disagreed with John Adams was Thomas Paine. Born in England in 1737, Paine had moved to the American colonies in 1774, after meeting Benjamin Franklin. There is a new spirit of independence in the colonies, Franklin said to Paine. In Europe, every man is subject to the king; but in America, things can be different; every man can decide his own destiny. Paine moved to Massachusetts and saw that Franklin was right—there was a greater sense of freedom in this "New World." The American colonists did see themselves as loyal subjects of the English king, George III, but a sense of individual freedom was emerging. The possibilities, it seemed, were endless.

Inspired by the independent spirit in the colonies' rebellion, Paine wrote a pamphlet called *Common Sense*, published in January 1776. It was very popular, ultimately becoming the best-selling document in America in the eighteenth century. *Common Sense* passionately argued for American independence from England, but, just as significant, *Common Sense* argued for "large and equal representation"[3] in the new government that would replace the old regime. By "large and equal representation," Paine meant that all citizens should have the right to vote, regardless of their gender and regardless of whether or not they were wealthy.

Paine's theories on suffrage were considered very radical. The debates about who should have the right to vote became too heated for the authors of the Constitution to handle. Was John Adams right—that only property owners should have suffrage? Or were Abigail Adams and Thomas Paine right—that all citizens should have suffrage?

Federalism

The founding fathers of the United States believed in dividing power between the federal government and the state governments. Federalism is a theory of government in which power is shared among two or more authorities rather than placed in the hands of only one authority. In a monarchy, the king or queen holds all the power. A monarchy is a system that can lead to abuses. What would prevent the monarch from doing whatever he or she wanted, regardless of the will of the people?

Throughout history, many nations realized that for freedom, liberty, and justice to flourish, governmental power must be divided. During 1787–1788, the early days of the United States, three of the founding fathers—James Madison, Alexander Hamilton, and John Jay—wrote *The Federalist Papers*. They asserted that a nation that shared power would ensure good government. The Constitution of the United States, then, is federalist in the sense that it directs power be shared between the federal government (located in the nation's capital) and the individual states. The authors of the Constitution decided to make suffrage a state right rather than a federal right. This decision would become very controversial in the decades following the ratification of the Constitution in 1789, especially when those citizens excluded from suffrage, specifically women and minorities, began to demand the right to vote.

The authors of the Constitution ultimately decided to do nothing about the issue. In the Constitution approved in 1789, there were no specific laws regarding suffrage. This was not an oversight by the founding fathers, but rather a strategy to leave voting rights to each individual state rather than in the hands of the federal government. This is known as federalism.

Though the U.S. Constitution in its original form in 1789 did not grant universal suffrage, the foundation had been laid by those who had spoken out in support of votes for women, such as Abigail Adams and Thomas Paine. Though women did not have the right to vote yet, the debates about women's suffrage had begun.

The French Revolution

In France, 1789 is known as *L'Année Cruciale*, that is, "The Crucial Year." As the United States had a few years earlier, France was experiencing its own revolution. After centuries of monarchy, the French people seized power and started a democracy, or government by the people. Influenced by the American Declaration of Independence, the French wrote their own document, *The Declaration of the Rights of Man and Citizen*. The foundations of the document were the ideas of "liberty, equality, and fraternity." In the new France, everyone was to have an equal chance at a good life. The document consisted of seventeen articles, most of which were about

Olympe de Gouges

One of the first women to argue for women's suffrage in France was Olympe de Gouges. The daughter of a butcher from southwest France, de Gouges moved to Paris as a teenager and became a writer. Excited by the possibilities in post-revolution France, in 1791 de Gouges wrote a pamphlet, *The Declaration of the Rights of Woman and Citizen*. Modeled after *The Declaration of the Rights of Man and Citizen*, de Gouges's *Declaration* also consisted of seventeen articles, each one mimicking the famous articles set down in 1789. De Gouges's *The Declaration of the Rights of Woman* argued that women should have the right to vote. It was one of the first documents to demand women's suffrage. She wrote her *Declaration* during a dangerous time in France, known as the "Reign of Terror." Between 1792 and 1794, tens of thousands of French citizens were killed by the guillotines in public spectacles. De Gouges was one of those victims. Because of her writings, she was labeled a troublemaker and sentenced to death. She was executed by guillotine on November 3, 1793.

the right of French citizens to govern themselves. The first declaration stated, "Men are born free and remain free and equal in rights."

Heavily influenced by the founding fathers in the United States, the French revolutionaries would soon gather to write their own constitution, a document that would bring democracy to France. And, as was true in America, the question of women's suffrage became an important topic. The first French Constitution, adopted in 1791, was primarily made to ensure that France would never again be ruled by a monarch. Women's suffrage did not seem such an important issue at the time. But French women had fought side-by-side with men during the French Revolution, so they wanted their voices heard in the new French government as well. Nevertheless, despite the protests of thousands of French women, France's new constitution excluded women from voting. As in America, French women would have a long wait for the right to vote.

Chapter 3

England and Early America

The French Revolution electrified the world, and perhaps nowhere more so than in England, one of France's closest neighbors. Many in England were excited by the spirit of freedom in France, excited by the promise of democracy. The French Revolution was not just a victory of the common people over the king. Due to the involvement of women during the revolution, now it was possible that everyone could help to change a country's government for the better. Though French women were denied the right to vote, the French Revolution, with its motto of "liberty, equality, and fraternity," still was viewed by some people as a sign that better times were on the way for women.

Mary Wollstonecraft

One of the first in England to see how the French Revolution could benefit women was Mary Wollstonecraft. Wollstonecraft was born in London in 1759, the second of six children. By the time Wollstonecraft was a teenager, she knew that she wanted to become a writer. But writing was a difficult profession, especially for women. Most people often saw women as less intelligent than men and were unlikely to read the work of a woman writer. Writing was an especially rough career choice for Mary Wollstonecraft, who had received very little formal schooling. But thanks to a famous public debate she had with England's most influential philosopher, Edmund Burke, Wollstonecraft earned a reputation as one of the great minds in Europe.

Wollstonecraft recognized that despite the democratic potential of the French Revolution, women were still excluded from politics. So, in 1792, she began to write her most famous work, *A Vindication of the Rights of Woman.*

During Wollstonecraft's lifetime, women were not considered to be intellectual creatures. Many, if not most, people believed that men were governed by reason, and women were governed by emotion. In *A Vindication of the Rights of Woman*, Wollstonecraft exposed those notions as prejudices. "I wish," Wollstonecraft wrote, "to persuade women to endeavour to acquire strength, both of mind and body."[1]

To Wollstonecraft, men had "deeply rooted prejudices" against women.[2] Furthermore, argued Wollstonecraft, men had invented those prejudices and

At Odds With Edmund Burke

One Englishman who was nervous about the French Revolution was Edmund Burke, a well-known writer and philosopher. In 1790, as the events of the revolution unfolded, Burke wrote a pamphlet called *Reflections on the Revolution in France*, in which he argued that the revolution was a bad idea. Burke contended that people who were not members of the upper class should know their place and stay out of government. Common people such as a hairdresser or a candle maker should have no say in government.

Though *Reflections* was popular, selling tens of thousands of copies immediately following its publication, many writers defended the French Revolution. One of the most important defenses was *A Vindication of the Rights of Men*, written by Mary Wollstonecraft in 1790. Though Wollstonecraft was unknown at the time, *Vindication* was a best seller and made her an overnight sensation. Her immediate fame was due not only to the fact that she had the bravery to argue with the most famous philosopher of the time. Her argument also was more reasoned, forceful, and compassionate than Burke's. She exposed Burke's *Reflections* as a defense of the privileges of the upper class. While Burke argued that aristocratic privileges were "natural" rights, Wollstonecraft argued that all men are born equal, so any rights they have are obtained throughout life rather used them to exclude women from government. Wollstonecraft believed that if women received the same education as men, then men and women could be equal partners in society.

Wollstonecraft's most radical suggestion in *A Vindication of the Rights of Woman*, however, was that women should have a voice in government. In Chapter IX of *Vindication*, she wrote, "women ought to have representatives, instead of being arbitrarily governed

This copy of Mary Wollstonecraft's *A Vindication of the Rights of Woman* was dedicated to the Library of Congress by Susan B. Anthony, an American for women's suffrage.

without having any direct share allowed them in the deliberations of government."[3] Wollstonecraft argued both that women should have a say in government and that women should be in government. These were very radical ideas at the time and would exert a tremendous amount of influence on the women's suffrage movement.

Today, historians see *A Vindication of the Rights of Woman* as very important and influential in the philosophy of women's rights. Many people during Wollstonecraft's lifetime, however, thought that she was dangerous. As a result, she was subject to a large amount of public abuse. One author, Horace Walpole, called her a "hyena in petticoats,"[4] and two books making fun of Wollstonecraft became best sellers: *A Vindication of the Rights of Brutes* and *A Sketch of the Rights of Boys and Girls*.

Conditions in England became so bad for Wollstonecraft that she left the country, spending most of the rest of her life in other European countries. She was known wherever she went, her work having been translated into many languages. She died in 1797, five years after the publication of *A Vindication of the Rights of Woman*, while giving birth to a daughter, Mary. Eventually, the younger Mary would also become a writer. She wrote the novel *Frankenstein*, published in 1818.

In the years following Mary Wollstonecraft's death,

A Vindication of the Rights of Woman would grow in importance. People realized that she was ahead of her time. Her work became important for women's rights in general and for women's suffrage in specific.

But it would be several decades after Mary Wollstonecraft's death before her pioneering work would bear fruit. Despite a growing sense that women were being deliberately kept out of government, real progress was slow in coming.

"The Cult of Domesticity"

John Adams had reminded his wife, Abigail, that the Declaration of Independence asserted only that "all *men* are created equal." However, there was a growing frustration in the United States with the fact that only men were involved in government. Many women wanted to be involved as well. Women's rights pioneers in Europe had given hope to American women, who now believed that the time was right for them to seek equal rights. In the first half of the nineteenth century, there were several important developments in America that would lay the foundation for women's voting rights.

Perhaps the biggest hurdle that women had to overcome was their traditional role throughout the centuries. At the beginning of the 1800s, women were trapped in a system some historians call "the cult of domesticity." This was a belief that women's lives should be limited to

33

their homes. According to the historian Martha J. Cutter, "[T]he predominant image for women in the early and middle nineteenth century was the Domestic Saint, an image which focused on women's attributes of piety [religiousness], purity, submissiveness, and domesticity."[5]

In short, "women were to live for others,"[6] not for themselves. This belief had widespread popularity in the United States and convinced many people that women should not be active in politics. Politics were reserved for men; women were to stay at home. The woman who submitted to the cult of domesticity was known as a "true woman."

In many ways, then, women in the nineteenth century were "locked" into domestic roles. But thanks to the work of women such as Olympe de Gouges and Mary Wollstonecraft, rumors were spreading that women could excel outside—as well as inside—their homes. But the cult of domesticity was very powerful: Many men *and* women argued that women should not be looking outside the home for fulfillment. A typical book of the 1800s assured women "that the surest pathway to the highest happiness and honor lies through the peaceful domain of wifehood and motherhood . . . To the true woman home is her throne."[7] Looking outside that "domain," it was believed, could only lead to trouble. Women who did not practice the "four cardinal virtues" (piety, purity, submissiveness, and domesticity) were

Godey's Lady's Book showed its interpretation of happiness for a woman in this 1850 illustration. This type of view was part of what some historians call the "cult of domesticity."

often punished. It was in this culture that the pioneers of the women's suffrage movement had to work, making their progress very difficult.

Emma Hart Willard

Not all women were happy with the cult of domesticity. Many American women in the first half of the nine-teenth century tried to break out of the roles society forced upon them. One of those women was Emma Hart Willard, who founded the Troy Female Seminary. Born in 1787 near Hartford, Connecticut, Emma Hart was the sixteenth of her father's seventeen children. At that time, American girls were given very little education. Most Americans even believed that girls were incapable of learning difficult subjects, such as geometry. But at age twelve, Emma taught herself geometry.[8] Knowing that other girls could learn difficult subjects, Emma dedicated her life to educating girls.

She began teaching while still a teenager. By age twenty, she was in charge of a boys' and girls' school in Vermont. She married a physician, Dr. John Willard, in 1809. In September 1821, Emma Hart Willard opened the Troy Female Seminary in Troy, New York. Troy Female Seminary was a radical school. There were girls' schools in America at that time, but they were known as "finishing schools." At these schools, teachers trained girls to be virtuous, obedient housewives. Emma Willard wanted her school to be different.

Willard believed that girls' studies should be just as demanding as those of boys'. According to historian Elisabeth Griffin:

> Willard was the first educator to replace the traditional offerings of female academies with a rigorous program of instruction. Although she called her school a "female seminary," she in fact aspired to make the classical and scientific curricula of men's colleges available to young women.[9]

In addition to religious and moral education, girls at Troy learned algebra, foreign languages, music, literature, philosophy, art, and psychology. Girls had been traditionally barred from most of those subjects.

Willard believed that, given the chance, girls could excel in the same difficult courses that schools offered boys. Willard, according to biographer John Lord, "was one of the first to demonstrate that there are no subjects

Emma Hart Willard

37

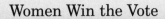

which young men can grasp which cannot equally be mastered by young ladies."[10] Willard's educational system became known as the "Troy plan." About two hundred schools modeled on the "Troy plan" opened all over the United States in the nineteenth century. Graduates of Troy Female Seminary founded many of these schools.[11]

The Troy Female Seminary was an important step forward in the women's rights movement. It supported Mary Wollstonecraft's belief that women deserved education equal to that of men. Though many Americans believed that "true women" must submit to the cult of domesticity, there were others who believed that true women could do other things, too.

Colleges for All

Another important milestone in the women's rights movement occurred just a few years later, when Oberlin College opened its doors to women. Two missionaries, John J. Shipherd and Philo P. Stewart, founded Oberlin College in northeast Ohio in 1833. They named the college in honor of Jean-Frederic Oberlin, a French missionary and philanthropist whom Shipherd and Stewart greatly admired. Shipherd and Stewart wanted their new college to be a shining light for reform. They knew that there were many things wrong in America—slavery was still legal, and women were trapped in their domestic roles. The two missionaries believed that Oberlin could make a difference and perhaps lead the way in reforming those problems.

In 1835, Oberlin became the first college to admit African-American men. Then, in 1837, Oberlin admitted its first women students—the first women undergraduates in the United States. Those four women were Mary Kellogg, Mary Caroline Rudd, Mary Hosford, and Elizabeth Prall. All but Kellogg earned their degrees, becoming, in 1841, the first women college graduates in the United States.

A few months after Oberlin began to admit women students, the Mount Holyoke Female Seminary opened on November 8, 1837. Located in South Hadley, Massachusetts, it was the first women's college in America. Founded by Mary Lyon, Mount Holyoke Female Seminary was a dramatic step forward in women's education. Like Emma Willard, Lyon believed that women should receive the same

Oberlin College became the first United States school to award college degrees to women.

Katharine Baldwin Sullivan painted this watercolor of Mary Lyon. According to notes on the back of the portrait, the watercolor was exhibited at the Mt. Holyoke department at the Chicago Exhibition of 1893.

education as men. Mount Holyoke used the same textbooks used at men's colleges, especially those for math and science, subjects that many believed women could not learn. Wishing to challenge the common prejudice that women could not master the sciences, Lyon required her students to take at least seven courses in math and science in order to graduate. Lyon herself taught chemistry.

Today, those three revolutionary institutions, Troy Female Seminary (now the Emma Willard School), Oberlin College, and Mount Holyoke College, are still in operation. They still carry the torch handed to them by Emma Willard, John J. Shipherd and Philo P. Stewart, and Mary Lyon.

For a long time, the cult of domesticity held a powerful grip on American women, convincing them that their duty was in the home—and in the home alone. By the 1840s, however, that grip was loosening. More and more women were seeking opportunities that did not exist before. Soon more girls' schools based on the "Troy plan" opened, and more colleges admitted women students. More important, those new schools produced women graduates who would become major players in reform movements, chief among them the abolition of slavery and the promotion of women's suffrage.

Chapter 4

The Seneca Falls Convention

The French and American revolutions promised a new hope for mankind that can be summed up in five words: "All men are created equal." Once those words were written, in both the American Declaration of Independence and in the French Declaration of the Rights of Man, the stage was set for dramatic social reforms. Two of the most important social-reform issues in the nineteenth century in the United States were the abolition of slavery and women's suffrage.

If everyone was created equal, then why in America did slavery still continue to exist, and why were women still excluded from suffrage? Soon after the American and French revolutions, reform societies emerged to deal with the inequality that still continued. In the United States, especially, concerned Americans formed several abolition societies. Some of the most famous were the Society for the Abolition of Slavery, the American Anti-Slavery

Society, and the Manumission (a word meaning "to free from slavery") Society. Women were among the most active members of these groups because they saw similarities between their living conditions and those of slaves. According to historian Alison Parker, "Those women who were drawn to abolitionism found a radical movement that spoke of freedom from oppression [and] natural inalienable rights."[1] One of the pioneers of the women's suffrage movement, Emily Collins, wrote, "All through the Anti-Slavery struggle, every word of denunciation of the wrongs of the Southern slave, was, I felt, equally applicable to the wrongs of my own sex. Every argument for the emancipation of the colored man, was equally one for that of woman."[2]

The rise of women's suffrage organizations in the United States was directly linked to the abolition movement. It was women's participation in abolition societies (and their newfound educational opportunities at schools such as Troy Seminary) that gave women the experience and confidence to launch the women's suffrage movement in America. So it should be no surprise that many of the pioneers of the women's suffrage movement were themselves prominent abolition activists.

A Girl Who Loved to Learn

One of the most famous of those women's suffrage pioneers was Elizabeth Cady Stanton. The eighth of

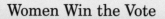

eleven children, Stanton was born in Johnstown, New York, in 1815, to Daniel and Margaret Cady. Daniel Cady was a successful lawyer who had served one term in the U.S. Congress. He ultimately achieved the position of New York Supreme Court justice. Despite the success of Daniel Cady, the Cady home was often filled with sadness. Five of Elizabeth's brothers and sisters died in early childhood.

Young Elizabeth was smart, curious, and energetic. Desiring to please her father, who was a learned man, Elizabeth wanted to learn everything that she could. Because Elizabeth showed a great deal of intelligence, her father sent her to a private tutor, Simon Hosack, who taught her Greek, mathematics, and chess. Those subjects were usually reserved for boys, but Elizabeth excelled at them. Even after her lessons were over, Elizabeth studied in her father's private library, reading every book she could find. It was in her father's large collection of law books that Elizabeth first learned about the oppression of slaves and women.

One legal case in particular made a lasting impression on young Elizabeth. One of the Cadys' neighbors, Flora Campbell, had saved up money to buy a farm. After purchasing the farm, she married and soon gave birth to a son. But Campbell's husband died suddenly, and the land was given to the young son, who had no interest in farming. Campbell was frustrated, demanding through the courts that the land be returned to her. She had bought the land herself and believed that she was the rightful landowner. But the court ruled in favor of the son.

Campbell went to Daniel Cady to seek legal advice. She had purchased the property with her own money, so why should ownership of the property go to her son when her husband died? With Elizabeth nearby listening to the conversation, Daniel Cady explained to Campbell that, according to New York law, when a property-owning woman marries, her land immediately becomes her husband's property. Furthermore, if he dies, the property falls into the hands of the nearest male heir. Pointing to the law in one of his books, Cady shrugged and said, "There's nothing I can do."

Infuriated, Elizabeth grabbed a knife from the kitchen and ran back to her father's library to cut out the offensive law from the book. Daniel Cady stopped her from cutting the page and gently explained that her actions would not make the law disappear. But memories of this incident remained with Elizabeth for the rest of her life. At that moment, she decided to devote her life to fighting discrimination.

At age fifteen, Elizabeth began attending the Troy Female Seminary. She excelled in her studies, moving toward the top of her class in every subject. Though she would become Troy's most famous student, she did not

finish her studies there. She left during her second year, returning home to a life of leisure.

Most girls, after finishing school, found husbands and settled down to quiet lives of servitude. And, indeed, it seemed as though that would be the path for Elizabeth. She was one of the best students in the history of Troy Female Seminary, but she had no opportunity for higher education. At that time, American women could not go to college. (Oberlin College would not allow women until 1837.) Frustrated by her lack of opportunity but resigned to her fate, Elizabeth spent the next few years doing the things that eligible young women traditionally did—attending parties, socials, and church. She never lost her love of learning and remained an avid reader for the rest of her life.

An Important Cause

Elizabeth Cady's life dramatically changed in 1839 when she started spending more time with her cousin, Gerrit Smith, in Peterboro, New York. Smith was the son of Cady's aunt. He was an intellectual with a powerful, instantly likeable personality. He was also one of the most important abolition activists in America during that time, serving as the president of the New York branch of the American Anti-Slavery Association, an office he held from 1836 to 1839.

Because of his political career, in which he had to work with people who had a wide range of political beliefs, Daniel Cady had forbidden his family to discuss abolition at home. At the Smith home, however, there was constant talk about the immorality of slavery. The Smith home was one of the centers of abolition activism in America. Many of the prominent abolitionists of the day were frequent houseguests. The atmosphere electrified Elizabeth Cady, who spent more time at the Smiths than at her own home. It was in the Smith home that she vowed to devote her life to the abolitionist cause.

It was also in the Smith home that Cady met a man named Henry Brewster Stanton, who, like Gerrit Smith, was a famous abolitionist. Stanton had gained fame as an antislavery activist in Ohio. In the early 1830s, as a student at Lane Seminary in Cincinnati, Stanton had led a walkout of fifty students who protested the school's anti-abolition policy. These fifty students, known as the "Lane Rebels," transferred to Oberlin College in Ohio. Stanton transferred to New York in the late 1830s to work as secretary of the American Anti-Slavery Association.

Elizabeth Cady and Henry Stanton fell in love immediately, and

This photo of Elizabeth Cady Stanton was taken in 1854.

within a month after first meeting, they were engaged. Cady's family was angry. They disapproved of the match on many counts. They felt that the couple had not known each other long enough to marry, and they did not like the fact that Stanton was poor. The Cadys also disapproved of Stanton's abolitionism. They thought that abolitionists were too radical.

Despite this, Cady married Stanton on May 1, 1840. She was twenty-four years old; he was thirty-five. Cady's parents did not attend the wedding, even though the ceremony occurred at their home. Stanton had a magnificent honeymoon planned for his wife. He was taking her to London, England, to attend the first World Anti-Slavery Convention, to be held in June 1840.

Stanton believed that the conference would strengthen his wife's dedication to the abolition cause. The conference, in fact, also spurred her to a deeper involvement in the women's rights movement.

A Turning Point

When the Stantons arrived in London, they stayed at the same boarding house as many of the women abolitionists. There, Elizabeth Cady Stanton met Lucretia Mott, a famous Quaker preacher. Quakers were a group of Christians who supported women's rights and allowed women to serve in leadership positions within their church.

Lucretia Mott

By the time of the World Anti-Slavery Convention in 1840, Lucretia Mott was already a famous activist. She was a member of The Society of Friends—also known as Quakers—which was one of the first religious organizations to permit women to occupy leadership positions. Mott was an intelligent, sensitive, and well-respected member of her Quaker church in Philadelphia. She was so respected, in fact, that she became a Quaker minister in 1818, at the age of twenty-eight. She was also an active abolitionist. Her home was a station along the Underground Railroad. (The Underground Railroad was a network of routes and safe houses that helped runaway slaves get to free states and to Canada in the 1800s.)

Convinced that women could have a powerful voice in ending slavery, in 1833, Mott founded the world's first women's abolition organization, the Philadelphia Female Anti-Slavery Society. Mott gained recognition as a persuasive public speaker. She toured the East Coast and Midwest, arguing for the abolition of slavery. By the time of the World Anti-Slavery Convention, Mott had gained the reputation for being one of the world's foremost abolitionists.

Lucretia Mott was a leading American abolitionist.

The World Anti-Slavery Convention opened on June 12, 1840, at the Freemason's Hall on Great Queen Street in London. Thomas Clarkson, an English abolitionist, was named president of the proceedings, and Henry Stanton was named secretary. There were five black delegates at the convention, all of whom were freed slaves: Henry Beckford and Louis Lecesne of Jamaica, Samuel Prescod of Barbados, M. L'Instant of Haiti, and Edward Barratt of the United States.

Though women were permitted to attend the World Anti-Slavery Convention, they could not serve as delegates, nor were they permitted to sit on the main floor of the convention hall. Instead, they were told to sit in a separate area at the end of the hall. They were even forced to sit behind a curtain while the convention took place. To Mott and Cady Stanton, this was an outrage. Women had worked side by side with men as antislavery activists. The women thought they should be permitted to serve as delegates, especially at such an important event.

The convention was not nearly as significant as its delegates hoped it would be. Though its agenda was to end slavery and the slave trade, its primary claim to fame turned out to be the exclusion of women participants. As delegate after delegate rose to defend barring women from participation, Cady Stanton and Mott grew more and more outraged. The two women rose from

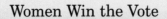

their seats and stormed out of the convention hall. Cady Stanton would write about this famous London walkout in her memoirs: "As Mrs. Mott and I walked away arm in arm, commenting on the incidents of the day, we resolved to hold a convention as soon as we returned home, and form a society to advocate the rights of women."[3] This conversation proved to be a significant early step toward equal rights. Though Cady Stanton and Mott planned to hold their women's rights convention soon after they returned home from England, the convention itself would have to wait eight years.

From Boston to New York

The Stantons were still a young newlywed couple when they returned to Johnstown, New York, a fact that delayed Cady Stanton's work as a women's rights activist. As soon as the Stantons got back from Europe, they started a family. Henry became a lawyer, working for a time as Daniel Cady's assistant until he opened up his own law practice in Boston in 1842. And just as Henry's career as an attorney began, so did Elizabeth's role as a mother. The Stantons' first child, Daniel Cady Stanton, was born in 1842; their second child, Henry B. Stanton, was born in 1844; and their third child, Gerrit Smith Stanton, was born in 1845.

Cady Stanton thrived in her role as mother, gaining additional confidence. She also was stimulated by the intellectual spirit in Boston. During her years in Boston, Cady Stanton met several famous people: writer and philosopher Ralph Waldo Emerson, novelist Nathaniel Hawthorne, poet John Greenleaf Whittier, composer Stephen Foster, and legendary abolitionist Frederick Douglass. Cady Stanton converted Douglass to the women's rights cause. Years later, Douglass would recall meeting Cady Stanton:

> I shall never forget how she unfolded her views
> to me on this question of the exclusion of women
> from having a hand in the governing of herself [. . .]
> Mrs. Stanton knew it was not only necessary to
> break the silence of women and make her voice
> heard, but woman must have a clear, palpable and
> comprehensive measure set before her, one worthy
> of her highest ambition and her best exertions.[4]

While in Boston, Cady Stanton continued her work as an abolitionist, all the while planning to follow up on her desire to hold a women's rights convention. However, two complications arose that further delayed the planned women's rights convention: Henry Stanton's and Lucretia Mott's health.

Though Henry was thriving as a well-respected Boston attorney, the Massachusetts climate did not agree with him. He was constantly ill with colds and persistent coughs. Though Henry did not wish to leave Boston, his health finally forced him to. As Cady Stanton noted in her memoirs, "As my husband's health was delicate, and the New England winters proved too severe for him, we left Boston with many regrets, and sought a more genial climate in Central New York."[5] In 1845, the Stantons moved to Seneca Falls, New York, a move that would prove beneficial to both Henry and Elizabeth.

Meanwhile, the trip to England had been quite stressful for Lucretia Mott. Upon returning to America, she became sick. According to historian Otelia Cromwell, "A sufferer from chronic dyspepsia [a stomach ailment], she became seriously ill shortly after her return from England; for a time her life was despaired of. As word of her illness spread, grave concern for her health was felt throughout the country."[6]

After several months of rest, Mott finally recovered. But tragedy struck Mott's family soon after her recovery. In 1844, Mott's mother, Anna Coffin, died, and in 1846 her brother, Thomas Coffin, also died. Though Mott was eager to follow up the promises she and Cady Stanton had made in London in 1840, she needed some time to recover.

Planning to Make History

For Mott and Cady Stanton, their dreams of a women's rights convention would come true in 1848. Even at that time, the memories of the women abolitionists' humiliation in London were still fresh in Elizabeth Cady Stanton's mind:

> My experience at the World's Antislavery
> Convention, all I had read of the legal status of
> women, and the oppression I saw everywhere,
> together swept across my soul, intensified now
> by many personal experiences. It seemed as if all
> the elements had conspired to impel me to some
> onward step. I could not see what to do or where to
> begin—my only thought was a public meeting for
> protest and discussion.[7]

By 1848, Mott had recovered her strength. In the summer, she was in the middle of an antislavery lecture tour. In the early summer, Cady Stanton received a letter from Martha Wright, Mott's sister, who lived nearby in Auburn, New York. Mott was coming to Auburn, so Wright invited Cady Stanton to visit in July. It had been eight years since Cady Stanton had met Mott, and she was eager to renew their friendship. They arranged a meeting at the home of Jane and Richard Hunt, Quaker friends of the Wrights, who lived in Waterloo, New York. That town was less than four miles from Seneca Falls.

Cady Stanton arrived in Waterloo on Thursday, July 13, 1848. She was delighted to find her dear friend

Lucretia Mott in good health, full of enthusiasm and energy. There were five women at the Hunt home that day: Elizabeth Cady Stanton, Lucretia Mott, Martha Wright, Jane Hunt, and Mary McClintock. Though the women were excited to make and renew friendships, the discussion soon focused on Mott and Cady Stanton's experience in London. Wright, Hunt, and McClintock were shocked by the story, and the women renewed Cady Stanton and Mott's original intent to organize a women's rights convention. All agreed that the convention should occur immediately, especially since Mott was in New York. She was one of the best-known abolitionists. Her famous name would draw people to the convention.

Today, conventions take as much as a year to plan and to organize—and that is with the modern conveniences of computers, cell phones, and airplanes. No such technological luxuries existed in 1848. However, the vision, energy, and courage of those five women enabled them to put together the convention in less than a week. They set the dates for the conference to be July 19–20, 1848. The convention was to begin only six days from the meeting at the Hunt home.

Two teams were organized. One group went to the newspaper to take out an advertisement. The other found a location for the conference. They wasted no time; both projects were completed by the end of the day on Thursday. They had convinced the minister of the Wesleyan Methodist Church in Seneca Falls to let them use the building for the convention. They also took out a small notice in the local paper, the *Seneca County Courier*:

> A convention to discuss the social, civil and religious
> condition and rights of woman, will be held in the
> Wesleyan Chapel, at Seneca Falls, N.Y., on
> Wednesday and Thursday the 19th and 20th
> of July current; commencing at 10 o'clock, a.m.
> During the first day the meeting will be exclusively
> for women, who are earnestly invited to attend.
> The public generally are invited to be present
> on the second day, when Lucretia Mott, of
> Philadelphia, and other ladies and gentlemen,
> will address the convention.[8]

Though the women were excited by the upcoming convention, they did not expect a large gathering. It was a hot summer, and Seneca Falls was a long distance from the centers of reform in America, especially New York City, Boston, and Philadelphia. Mott wrote a letter to Cady Stanton on July 16, saying, "The convention will not be so large as it otherwise might be, owing to the busy time with the farmers' harvest."[9] But word of the convention spread quickly, and as July 19 dawned,

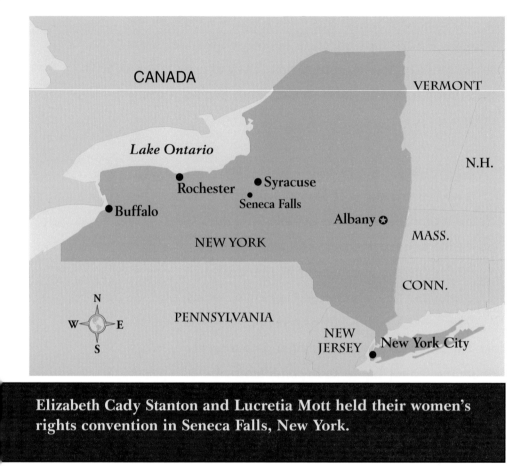

Elizabeth Cady Stanton and Lucretia Mott held their women's rights convention in Seneca Falls, New York.

hundreds of people descended on the small town of Seneca Falls.

A Landmark Meeting

The convention began at precisely 10 A.M. Only women were allowed to enter the church. Mott's husband, James Mott, was the lone exception to the women-only rule. In traditional parliamentary procedure, a chairman calls the proceedings to order. Desiring legitimacy for the convention, the women delegates asked James Mott to call the meeting to order.

Dozens of men surrounded the church, peering into the windows and listening at the doors, grumbling at their exclusion. The doors having been ceremoniously locked, Lucretia Mott began reading the convention's Declaration of Sentiments. This document, modeled after the Declaration of Independence, aired the grievances that women had been enduring for centuries. In the Declaration of Independence, the founding fathers had written, "We hold these truths to be self-evident: that all men are created equal." The women of the Seneca Falls Convention, however, announced in their declaration, "We hold these truths to be self-evident: that all men and women are created equal." Adding the words "and women" was a bold move, resulting in murmurs of approval from the approximately one hundred women in the church.

What followed in the 976-word Declaration of Sentiments were grievances regarding the historic mistreatment of women and about men's refusal to grant equal treatment to women, who were seen as "the weaker sex." Another grievance read, "He has denied her the facilities for obtaining a thorough education, all colleges being closed against her."[10] As the fifteen grievances were read, a man crawled through one of the church

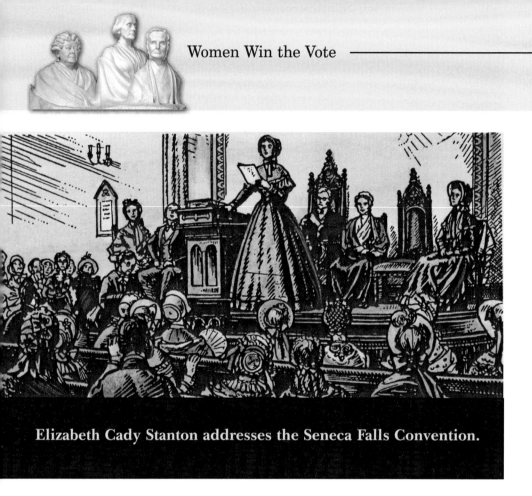

Elizabeth Cady Stanton addresses the Seneca Falls Convention.

windows and fell into the building. He then unlocked the door, and men filed into the church. Several women demanded that the men leave immediately.

Not wanting to repeat the exclusion that they themselves had suffered for so long, the women ultimately agreed to allow the men to remain. Cady Stanton recalled, "it was decided, in hasty council round the altar, that this was an occasion when men might make themselves pre-eminently useful." Soon the building was crowded with men and women. They were packed shoulder-to-shoulder in the pews and standing elbow-to-elbow in the aisles. There were too many for the church to accommodate. Many people were still forced to stand outside, hoping to hear the proceedings.

After the Declaration of Sentiments was read, another document was announced: the Resolutions. The purpose of the Declaration was to list the grievances that women had regarding their mistreatment. The purpose of the Resolutions was to propose solutions to the grievances. Mott read the twelve resolutions, the first being "*Resolved*, That such laws as conflict, in any way with the true and substantial happiness of woman, are contrary to the great precept of nature and of no validity, for this is 'superior in obligation to any other.'"

The crowd met all but one of the twelve resolutions with applause and shouts of approval. But when the ninth resolution was read, a hush fell over the crowd: "*Resolved*, That it is the duty of the women of this country to secure to themselves their sacred right to the elective franchise." This was the boldest of the convention's resolutions. Many in the audience—both men and women—opposed the suggestion that women should have "the elective franchise," that is, the right to vote. The momentary silence was broken by Mott, who dutifully read the remaining three resolutions. She then announced that the convention would vote on each resolution the following day.

A break was then announced, and everyone filed out

of the church. It was an extraordinary event. Many in the crowd realized that they were on the wave of a revolution. But the real topic of conversation—the real controversy—among the crowd was Resolution 9. The issue of women's suffrage dominated the convention for the remainder of the two-day conference.

As July 19 ended, Cady Stanton grew concerned. She knew that men would be adamantly opposed to women's suffrage, just as men had been opposed to it during the American and French revolutions. Cady Stanton was shocked that many women at the convention were opposed to women's suffrage as well. She feared that when the convention voted on the resolutions, Resolution 9 might be rejected, a possibility that filled her with dread. To make matters worse, her own husband was against Resolution 9!

Furthermore, at that time, Cady Stanton did not feel confident as a public speaker. Though she was bold, intelligent, and courageous, she had not yet developed public-speaking skills. Fortunately for the cause of women's suffrage, one of the most famous public speakers in America was at the Seneca Falls Convention—Frederick Douglass. Cady Stanton approached Douglass to ask for help. She herself had converted Douglass to the women's suffrage cause when they had met in Boston five years earlier. Douglass had traveled fifty miles from his home in Rochester, New

York, to be involved in this momentous convention, and he was eager to help out. He assured her that when the time came to vote, he would do all he could to secure the passage of Resolution 9.

At 10 A.M. on July 20, the convention resumed. The order of business was to vote first on the Declaration of Sentiments. The women delegates passed it unanimously. Everyone was looking forward to the evening session when the convention would vote on the resolutions, especially the now-controversial Resolution 9. At 7 P.M., the Wesleyan Methodist Church was packed, with even more people jammed into the building than had been there for the previous session. Everyone knew it was a historic occasion. But were they at the dawn of a new age—when men and women could vote together—or would the old order win the day?

The first eight resolutions passed unanimously. And then Mott began to read Resolution 9 before a crowd hushed in anticipation. According to parliamentary procedure, when a resolution is announced, someone must "make a motion" to adopt the resolution. After that motion, another person has to "second" the motion, meaning that at least two people must approve of the motion before the rest of the people can vote on it. After Resolution 9 was read, Cady Stanton, to no one's surprise, rose to move that the resolution be approved. She then sat down, hoping that someone would rise to second

This rare photo of Frederick Douglass (to left of table) shows him at an anti-Fugitive Slave Act convention in Cazenovia, New York, on August 22, 1850. The man standing behind Douglass is thought to be Gerrit Smith. The woman with the bonnet in the center may be Abigail Kelley Foster, who first urged Susan B. Anthony to become an abolitionist speaker.

the motion. A long, uncomfortable silence followed. Would anyone have the courage to second the motion?

After a few tense moments, Frederick Douglass slowly rose to second the motion. The crowd was amazed. Douglass, a former slave and an abolitionist speaker, was one of the most famous men in America, and here he was proudly arguing for women to have the right to vote. In his bold, powerful voice, he proclaimed, "The power to choose rulers and make laws is the right by which all others could be secured."[11]

Resolution 9 passed. This was a wonderful moment for Cady Stanton. Eight years earlier, she had been forced to sit mute in the Freemason's Hall in London, unable to speak out against the evils of slavery because she was a woman. And now, a prominent American, Frederick Douglass, had supported the passage of Resolution 9 at the Seneca Falls Convention. At that moment, the partnership of the abolition and women's suffrage movements was solidified. The cause of women's suffrage had made a crucial step forward.

Chapter 5

More Women Seek the Vote

The passage of the 1848 Seneca Falls Convention resolutions, particularly Resolution 9, was an important moment in the history of women's suffrage. The passage of those resolutions, however, did not grant women the right to vote. After the Seneca Falls Convention, Elizabeth Cady Stanton and Lucretia Mott were now the leading pioneers in women's suffrage. However, even though Cady Stanton and Mott were energetic and charismatic figures, more activists were needed.

Fortunately for the cause of women's suffrage, a strong wave of activists would come forward after Seneca Falls. Many of them, like Cady Stanton and Mott, came from the abolition movement. In 1848, only white men could vote and slavery was still legal, so there was still much work to be done. At the crest of that wave of activism was one of the most important people in American history: Susan B. Anthony.

A Supportive Upbringing for a Future Leader

Susan Brownell Anthony was born on February 15, 1820, in Adams, Massachusetts, the third of Daniel and Lucy Anthony's eight children. Like Lucretia Mott, the Anthonys were Quakers and abolitionists. Susan enjoyed a healthy, normal childhood. In 1826, the Anthony family moved to Battenville, New York (about thirty-five miles north of Albany) so that Daniel Anthony could manage a factory.

Young Susan was sent to the local district school. Though little was expected of girls academically in those days, Susan was very intelligent and excelled in her studies. She soon proved herself the smartest student in her class. Not long after she started school, however, the teacher refused to teach the girls long division. The teacher insisted that girls were not smart enough to learn such difficult math. Susan stormed home in a fit of anger and told her father.

Susan was fortunate to have a father such as Daniel Anthony. He was a Quaker who believed that women were men's equals. Wishing his daughters to receive the best possible education, Daniel Anthony withdrew Susan and her older sister Guelma from the district school and decided to teach his daughters at home. His work as a factory manager was time-consuming, however, so before

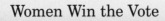

long he hired a full-time teacher for the Anthony "home school." That teacher was Mary Perkins. Though public schools in America at that time were more interested in teaching "the feminine morality of humility and piety"[1] to girls, Perkins believed that girls should receive the same strict education as boys.

Susan succeeded in her studies. When she turned seventeen, she began attending Deborah Moulson's Female Seminary, a Quaker boarding school, near Philadelphia, Pennsylvania. Though the Moulson school, like many "finishing schools," was primarily interested in teaching morality, it nevertheless included rigorous training in algebra, accounting, literature, chemistry, philosophy, and anatomy.

The headmistress, Deborah Moulson, believed that in order for girls to become religious, serious adults, they must be constantly humiliated. Soon after arriving at school, Susan felt the full effect of Moulson's teaching style. One day, Susan had finished a handwriting exercise, and, eager to please Moulson, she rushed up to the front of class to show her the paper. Fully expecting praise for her beautiful, careful handwriting, Susan instead heard Moulson say, "Obviously, Susan, you do not know the rule for dotting 'i's. I have devoted my time to you in vain."[2] Susan was crushed and returned to her desk.

Susan suffered more such humiliations. But life was not always miserable for Susan at school. She was fortunate to make friends with Lydia Mott, the niece of Lucretia Mott. Lydia was a good, loyal friend. Because she was a student at Moulson, her famous aunt often came to the school to lecture the girls on intellectual development and civic responsibility. Lucretia Mott's lectures, filled with hope and respect, were quite different than the oppressive style of Moulson. They impressed the young mind of Susan Anthony, who by then was growing more sensitive to issues of social justice.

Susan did not endure the harsh environment of Moulson for long. Before her first year was finished, Susan was called home. A financial crisis had gripped the nation in 1837, and the Anthony home was one of its victims. Daniel Anthony had suffered financial ruin and could no longer afford Susan's schooling.

From Teacher to Activist

To help pay off her father's massive debts, Susan B. Anthony became a schoolteacher. In 1839, she took her first job, at Kenyon's Friends' Seminary, a Quaker school, in New Rochelle, New York. The headmistress, Eunice Kenyon, was an easy-going, cheerful woman—a stark contrast to Deborah Moulson. Kenyon urged Anthony to explore her own style of teaching, a fact that surprised Anthony. New Rochelle was not far from New

York City, and Anthony occasionally went to the city to attend temperance or abolition lectures.

In 1846, the twenty-six-year-old Anthony took a position as headmistress of girls' education at the Canajoharie Academy in Canajoharie (a Mohawk Indian word, pronounced "Can-uh-juh-HARE-ee"), New York. The town was halfway between Albany and Utica. Anthony was a good teacher. She demanded a lot from her students, but she did not believe in the berating, humiliating style of Deborah Moulson. She taught the same subjects as were taught at Moulson but in the more easy-going style learned from Kenyon.

While living in Canajoharie, Anthony began her career as an activist. Canajoharie was not far from the home of her old school friend, Lydia Mott, who lived with her sister Abigail in Albany. Anthony often visited the Mott sisters, who, because of their connection to their famous aunt, Lucretia Mott, were actively involved in various reform movements. In 1848, the New York Property Bill was amended to allow women partial property rights. Although the Mott sisters were

Susan B. Anthony was soon drawn into the abolition movement. It was there that she would meet some of her key allies in the fight for the right to vote.

Temperance

From the earliest days in the United States, alcoholism was a problem. In the American colonies, more and more people left their farms and moved to places such as New York City, Boston, and Philadelphia. Because work was not always available to the large influx of people, problems such as poverty, crime, domestic violence, and alcoholism increased dramatically in the cities. As a result of the rise of alcoholism, temperance (a word meaning "moderation") organizations began to appear, especially in the large urban centers. One of the first temperance activists was Dr. Benjamin Rush. He was a well-respected physician and one of the signers of the Declaration of Independence. In 1805, Rush wrote a paper entitled "The Effects of Ardent Spirits Upon Man." Many people read this paper, which launched the temperance movement in America. Before long, temperance organizations appeared all over the United States. These included the American Society for the Promotion of Temperance, the Daughters of Temperance, the American Temperance Society, and the Templars of Honor and Temperance.

Women were often indirectly the hardest hit by alcoholism, when men in their lives became victims of the disease. Because of this, the temperance movement was one of the first social movements in which women fully participated. Furthermore, because of their experience as powerful voices within the movement, many women temperance activists—such as Lucretia Mott, Susan B. Anthony, and Elizabeth Cady Stanton—were also influential in the abolition and women's rights movements.

excited by this monumental reform in the New York legal system, they believed it was only a start toward larger, more dramatic reforms. That summer was also the summer of the Seneca Falls Convention, which had brought recognition to Lucretia Mott and Elizabeth Cady Stanton. At the Mott home, Anthony would meet many of the pioneers of the women's rights movement.

Soon after arriving in town, Anthony joined an organization called the Daughters of Temperance. Temperance was a reform movement that sought to reduce the consumption of alcoholic beverages.

Though a newcomer to town, Anthony quickly proved herself a likable, confident, and energetic member, and rose quickly to the office of secretary. More important, it was as a member of the Daughters of Temperance that Anthony began to make her reputation as a bold, forceful public speaker. On March 1, 1849, the Daughters of Temperance invited all the townspeople to attend a formal dinner. Anthony was the featured speaker. As she was escorted to the front of the hall, she saw a large banner posted on the wall behind the speaker's stand. It read in large letters, "Susan B. Anthony."

In the nineteenth century, it was rare for a woman to speak in public. Women public speakers were often openly ridiculed by men during their speeches and then subject to further insult in the following days' newspapers. But standing before the two hundred audience members that evening, Anthony showed no sign of nerves or fear. Her speech was a rousing success. Both men and women cheered her afterward, hailing Anthony as "the smartest woman who has ever been in Canajoharie."

Anthony had found her activist calling. One month later, she resigned from the Canajoharie Academy and moved back to Rochester. She continued her work as a temperance activist and enlisted in the abolition cause as well. Rochester was not only the home of the Anthony family; it was also the home of Frederick Douglass. Douglass's antislavery newspaper, *The North Star*, was published in Rochester. The city was a stop along the Underground Railroad, with an estimated 150 escaped slaves coming through town each year. Indeed, the city was known as one of the centers of the abolition cause in America. Anthony's father introduced her to Douglass soon after her arrival. They became instant friends and would remain so for the rest of their lives. Impressed by the larger-than-life Douglass, Anthony soon joined the American Anti-Slavery Society.

In the spring of 1851, Anthony traveled to Syracuse, New York, to attend an antislavery convention. On her way back to Rochester, Amelia Bloomer, a fellow temperance activist, invited Anthony to visit her home in Seneca Falls. The town had gained notoriety since the famous convention three years earlier. As a result, it was

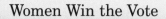

a popular stop on various lecture tours. That spring, two famous abolitionists, American William Lloyd Garrison and Englishman George Thompson, would deliver anti-slavery lectures at Seneca Falls. Also attending the lectures was a woman who would forever change Anthony's life: Elizabeth Cady Stanton.

Frederick Douglass had spoken warmly about Cady Stanton, and Anthony was eager to meet her. And there on the street, after the evening's lectures, Bloomer introduced Cady Stanton to Anthony. In her memoirs, Cady Stanton recalled her first impression of Anthony: "There she stood with her good, earnest face and genial smile."[3] They could not have foreseen it at the time, but this introduction would blossom into one of the most famous friendships in American history.

Despite their now-famous meeting in 1851, Anthony and Cady Stanton did not become close friends until several months later. At that time, the two women met with Lucy Stone in order to make plans for a coeducational college in New York. Lucy Stone was one of the first women to have a college education, having graduated

Lucy Stone graduated from Oberlin College.

from Oberlin College in 1847. Like Anthony and Cady Stanton, Stone was a tireless advocate for abolition and women's rights. Though Cady Stanton had become widely known because of the local Seneca Falls Convention, it was Lucy Stone who had organized the first national women's rights convention, held in Worcester, Massachusetts, in 1850. As these three women sat in the parlor of the Stanton home, they were doing more than making plans to bring college education to New York women. They were laying the foundation for women's suffrage in America. According to biographer Ida Husted Harper:

> This was Miss Anthony's first meeting with Lucy Stone and may be called the commencement of her life-long friendship with Mrs. Stanton. These women who sat at the dinner-table that day were destined to be recorded in history for all time as the three central figures in the great movement for equal rights.[4]

Though the women were unsuccessful in their attempts to launch a New York coeducational college, those meetings solidified the friendship among the three women. Anthony and Cady Stanton, in fact, became best friends and forged a bond that would ultimately help to bring suffrage to American women.

African-American Women Lend Their Voices

The 1850s were a difficult time in American history. There were growing tensions between the free northern states and the slaveholding southern states. Slave owners in the South, who held a large amount of political power, were angry that so many slaves were escaping to the North. Not wanting civil war to erupt, Congress intervened in 1850. The government enacted the Fugitive Slave Law as part of a larger compromise known as the Compromise of 1850. The Fugitive Slave Law called for northern law officials to return runaway slaves to the South. Immediately after the passage of the law, thousands of former slaves—many of whom had been in the North for years[5]—were rounded up and sent back to their former owners.

With the enactment of the Fugitive Slave Law, abolitionists and women's rights advocates saw more clearly the need to be unified in their efforts. Slavery, after all, was not limited to men. African-American women were just as interested in women's rights as they were in abolition. This bond would draw together white and black abolitionists to form a powerful partnership in the struggle for women's rights. The Fugitive Slave Law, which was seen as a shocking violation of human rights, drew together the circles of abolition and women's rights activists.

One of the early leaders of that partnership was the former slave Sojourner Truth. Born into slavery as Isabella Baumfree in Swartekill, New York, around 1797, she was sold as a slave three times before escaping to freedom in 1826. In 1843, she changed her name to Sojourner Truth and began her career as an abolition and women's rights activist. Unlike many white women activists, Truth was very poor and had to support herself as a domestic servant while she traveled from town to town. She cleaned homes during the day and delivered abolition lectures in the evenings. People often fiercely opposed her lectures. Not only was it rare for a woman to speak publicly, but an African-American woman faced the double hurdles of racism and misogyny (the hatred of women). Many times during her lectures, Truth's voice was drowned out by boos, catcalls, and racist insults. Those same crowds, however, were often won over by her courage and powerful speaking style. By 1851, she had published her autobiography, *The Narrative of Sojourner Truth: A Northern Slave*, and enjoyed the well-earned reputation as a great public speaker.

Sojourner Truth was not alone in her efforts as an African-American woman activist. Harriet Forten Purvis and Margaretta Forten, the daughters of a wealthy Philadelphia merchant named James Forten, were

Sojourner Truth was a powerful speaker who voiced her support for abolition and women's rights.

influential abolitionists and women's rights activists who helped found the interracial Philadelphia Female Anti-Slavery Society. Mary Ann Shadd Cary founded the abolition newspaper *The Provincial Freeman* in 1853. Sarah Parker Remond was a brilliant woman who, because of racial and sexist prejudice in America, had to travel to Italy to earn her medical degree. She was a strong speaker at many of the women's rights conventions. The 1850s were a vibrant time for the growing women's rights movement. It was clear that, at the time, the causes of abolition and women's suffrage were linked hand-in-hand. It was also clear that the African-American voice was crucial in the fight for women's suffrage.

Many African-American abolitionists and women's rights activists were frustrated by racial prejudice within the women's rights movement. To many white activists, women's rights meant white women's rights.[6] Susan B. Anthony, however, saw her African-American colleagues as full partners. In a famous incident in 1861, Anthony and Frederick Douglass together hung a large banner from the Rochester, New York, Corinthian Hall. It read "No compromise with slaveholders."[7] This slogan served as a rallying cry for the abolition cause and also drew thousands of men and women—both black and white—into the women's suffrage cause.

Chapter 6

Battles Lost and Won

In the 1850s and 1860s, women's rights activists worked together with abolitionists to bring universal suffrage to the United States. Shortly after the victory of the North had ended the Civil War in 1865, Congress passed the Thirteenth Amendment. This change to the Constitution abolished slavery. One order of business in post-war America, then, was to amend the Constitution so that African Americans could vote. But did that mean *all* African Americans, or just African-American *men*? Because women had been such powerful figures in the abolition movement, it was hoped that a new constitutional amendment would include all women as voters.

In 1866, Susan B. Anthony, Elizabeth Cady Stanton, Lucy Stone, and Frederick Douglass organized the American Equal Rights Association (AERA). The stated agenda of the AERA was gender and racial equality. One of the AERA's projects was to make sure that suffrage was granted to African Americans but also to make sure any constitutional amendment would also include women.

In 1868, Anthony and Cady Stanton founded their own reform newspaper, *The Revolution*. Its motto was "Men their rights and nothing more; women their rights, and nothing less." Together with the AERA, *The Revolution* pressured the U.S. Congress to include women in the Fifteenth Amendment. There was, indeed, great hope that women would now receive the right to vote.

In February 1869, Congress proposed the Fifteenth Amendment to the U.S. Constitution: "The right of citizens of the United States to vote shall not be denied or abridged by the United States or any State on account of race, color or condition of previous servitude." Though this was hailed as a victory in the African-American community, women's rights activists were stunned. Why wasn't "or gender" added to the list of categories not to be denied? The Fifteenth Amendment, in other words, was, if ratified, going to grant suffrage to African-American men, but not to women—not African-American women, not any women.

The AERA, at its third-anniversary convention in May 1869, met in New York to discuss the Fifteenth Amendment. Douglass, much to the surprise of many of the women present, made a resolution to "welcome the pending Fifteenth Amendment prohibiting

A PETITION

FOR

UNIVERSAL SUFFRAGE.

To the Senate and House of Representatives:

The undersigned, Women of the United States, respectfully ask an amendment of the Constitution that shall prohibit the several States from disfranchising any of their citizens on the ground of sex.

In making our demand for Suffrage, we would call your attention to the fact that we represent fifteen million people—one half the entire population of the country—intelligent, virtuous, native-born American citizens; and yet stand outside the pale of political recognition.

The Constitution classes us as "free people," and counts us *whole* persons in the basis of representation; and yet are we governed without our consent, compelled to pay taxes without appeal, and punished for violations of law without choice of judge or juror.

The experience of all ages, the Declarations of the Fathers, the Statute Laws of our own day, and the fearful revolution through which we have just passed, all prove the uncertain tenure of life, liberty and property so long as the ballot—the only weapon of self-protection—is not in the hand of every citizen.

Therefore, as you are now amending the Constitution, and, in harmony with advancing civilization, placing new safeguards round the individual rights of four millions of emancipated slaves, we ask that you extend the right of Suffrage to Woman—the only remaining class of disfranchised citizens—and thus fulfil your Constitutional obligation "to Guarantee to every State in the Union a Republican form of Government."

As all partial application of Republican principles must ever breed a complicated legislation as well as a discontented people, we would pray your Honorable Body, in order to simplify the machinery of government and ensure domestic tranquillity, that you legislate hereafter for persons, citizens, tax-payers, and not for class or caste.

For justice and equality your petitioners will ever pray.

NAMES.	RESIDENCE.
Elizabeth Stanton	New York
Susan B. Anthony	Rochester—N.Y.
Antoinette Brown Blackwell	New York
Lucy Stone	Newark N. Jersey
Joanna S. Morse	48 Livingston. Brooklyn
Ernestine L. Rose	New York
Harriet E. Eaton	6, West 14th Street N.Y.
Catharine C. Wilkeson	83 Clinton Place New York
Elizabeth R. Tilton	48 Livingston St. Brooklyn
Mary Fowler Gilbert	295 W. 19" St New York
Amy E. Gilbert	New York
M. Griffith	New York.

In 1866, Elizabeth Cady Stanton, Susan B. Anthony, and Lucy Stone wrote "A Petition for Universal Suffrage" to Congress asking for a women's suffrage amendment to the Constitution.

disenfranchisement on account of race and earnestly solicit the State legislatures to pass it without delay."[1] Many of the African-American women present at the convention felt betrayed. The proposed amendment would exclude them from suffrage because of their gender. Despite this, Douglass believed that it was better to only grant suffrage to African-American men than to have no constitutional amendment at all. Anthony rose to protest the resolution: "The business of this association is to demand for every man, black or white, and every woman, black or white, that they shall be enfranchised and admitted into the body politic with equal rights and privileges."[2]

After much heated debate, the AERA voted to support Douglass's resolution. This outraged many of the women present. On the very last day of the convention, the Woman's Bureau of the AERA met to discuss these controversial events. Many of them wanted no further part of the AERA. They felt that women, who had been among the most loyal crusaders in the abolition movement, were now being left out of the reforms once slavery had been abolished.

At that meeting, held on May 15, 1869, Susan B. Anthony, Elizabeth Cady Stanton, and Lucy Stone formed the National Women's Suffrage Association (NWSA). They launched a nationwide lecture tour, hoping to rally support to pressure Congress to include

The Reconstruction Amendments

Between 1865 and 1870, the U.S. Congress ratified three Constitutional Amendments, today known as the "Reconstruction Amendments." The Thirteenth Amendment, passed in 1865, ended slavery. The Fourteenth Amendment, passed in 1868, granted full citizenship to former slaves. The Fifteenth Amendment, passed in 1870, granted voting rights to African-American men. Perhaps the most profound of the Reconstruction Amendments was the Fourteenth, which included a "citizenship" paragraph: "All persons born or naturalized in the United States, and subject to the jurisdiction thereof, are citizens of the United States." This paragraph would prove significant to women's suffrage advocates because, after women were excluded from suffrage in the Fifteenth Amendment, they attempted to use the "citizenship" paragraph in the Fourteenth Amendment to argue for the vote.[3] Their argument was that because they were "citizens" according to the Constitution, they should be granted full legal rights—especially the right to vote.

women in the Fifteenth Amendment. Anthony and Cady Stanton's newspaper, *The Revolution*, continued to carry articles about women's suffrage. Thousands of men and women wrote letters of protest to their congressmen, and the lecture tour rallied support for the women's suffrage cause.

But not everyone present at the birth of the NWSA was happy. Believing that the NWSA was too radical, Lucy Stone withdrew from the organization and formed the American Women's Suffrage Association (AWSA) in November 1869. The AWSA believed that women's suffrage could be achieved through federalism rather than through a constitutional amendment. In other words, the AWSA thought that if they could convince individual states to adopt women's suffrage first, then nationwide

Susan B. Anthony and Elizabeth Cady Stanton stand on a platform during a meeting of the National Women's Suffrage Association in the 1870s.

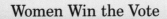

suffrage would happen eventually. In her initial letter to form the AWSA, Stone wrote:

> The undersigned, being convinced of the necessity for an American Women's Suffrage Association, which shall embody the deliberate action of the State organizations, and shall carry with it their united weight, do hereby respectfully invite such organizations to be represented in a Delegate Convention.[4]

Stone was concerned that there was too much bitterness between Southern congressmen, who rabidly opposed the Fifteenth Amendment, and Northern congressmen, many of whom had been involved in abolition movements. With so much infighting in the halls of the U.S. Congress, Stone believed that the best chance for women's suffrage would be to pressure individual state legislatures—the Northern states first, of course—to adopt women's suffrage. The highest profile members of the AWSA were Lucy Stone; her husband, Henry Blackwell; Julia Ward Howe; and Henry Ward Beecher (the AWSA's first president).

On February 3, 1870, the Fifteenth Amendment to the U.S. Constitution was ratified. African-American men were now "enfranchised," meaning that for the first time, they could vote. The abolition movement had

Lucy Stone

Lucy Stone was born on August 13, 1818, on a farm near West
Brookfield, Massachusetts. As a teenager, she learned that Oberlin
College in Ohio would be the first American college to admit women
students. Receiving no help from her parents, Stone saved for nine
years to attend Oberlin. She was one of the first women in the United
States to earn a college degree, graduating from Oberlin in 1847.
In 1850, inspired by the Seneca Falls Convention, Stone organized
the first National Woman's Rights Convention, in Worcester,
Massachusetts.

In 1855, Stone married the antislavery activist Henry
Blackwell. The marriage became a national scandal when Stone
refused to adopt her husband's last name. For decades afterwards,
women who kept their own last names were known as "Lucy
Stoners." After forming the American Women's Suffrage Association
in 1869, Stone founded *The Woman's Journal*, which was a powerful
instrument in the women's suffrage movement. Like her friends
Susan B. Anthony and Elizabeth Cady Stanton, Stone would die
before American women were granted the right to vote, but she
was one of the most influential architects of the women's suffrage
movement.

succeeded—slavery was outlawed and African-American men could vote. Nevertheless, hopes that women's suffrage would be part of the post-abolition reforms were dashed. It was a devastating setback for the women's suffrage movement. However, because of the formation of the NWSA and the ASWA, a wave of public support for women's suffrage began to build.

One of the first radical steps occurred in 1872, the presidential-election year following the passage of the Fifteenth Amendment. Stifled by the Fifteenth Amendment, Susan B. Anthony attempted to challenge a clause in the Fourteenth Amendment in order to vote in the election. On the morning of November 1, 1872, in Rochester, New York, Anthony marched with her two sisters, Guelma McLean and Hannah Mosher, to the voter registration station at the local barber shop. The men at the registration table glared at the women. "I demand that you register us as voters," said Anthony calmly. The men refused.

"If you still refuse us our rights as citizens," Anthony said, standing her ground, "I will bring charges against you in Criminal Court and I will sue each of you personally for large, exemplary damages."[5]

The men still turned Anthony and her sisters away. But three days later, Anthony and fourteen other women snuck into the voting station and cast their ballots. Three weeks later, Anthony was arrested for illegal voting. It was an international sensation. Newspapers all across the country described Anthony's attempt to vote. *The New York Times* headline blazed "Female Suffrage—The Case of Miss Anthony."[6] The news crossed the Atlantic Ocean. *The London Times* ran a story on "the conviction of Miss Susan B. Anthony, a famous advocate of Women's Rights, of having violated the election laws by voting in the November election."[7]

Anthony's goal in attempting to vote in the 1872 election was to "invoke" the first paragraph of the Fourteenth Amendment to the U.S. Constitution, which granted full citizenship to anyone "born or naturalized in the United States." If American women were "born" in America, shouldn't they be granted a citizenship right such as the right to vote? Anthony was indeed hoping to be arrested. If she were convicted of illegal voting in the New York courts, then she could appeal the ruling to the Supreme Court. The Supreme Court determines the validity of local, state, and federal laws. But the New York Supreme Court prevented her from taking her case to the U.S. Supreme Court. This was another bitter blow to the women's suffrage movement. Because the Fourteenth Amendment would not get challenged in the Supreme Court, a new Constitutional amendment would have to be sought. After 1872, Anthony marched to the halls of Congress almost every year to demand a Sixteenth Amendment: "The rights of citizens of the

African-American Women's Organizations

Mary Ann
Shadd Cary

In the nineteenth century, there was perhaps no group of people in the United States more united in the causes of abolition and suffrage than African-American women. African-American women had actually experienced the double sting of slavery and antisuffrage.

Beginning in the 1880s, African-American women began organizing local suffrage groups. Mary Ann Shadd Cary, publisher of the abolition journal *The Provincial Freeman*, founded The Colored Women's Progressive Franchise Association, based in Washington, D.C., in 1880. The organization's three foundations were "Demand equal rights," "Reject the idea that only men conduct industrial and other enterprises," and "Obtain the ballot."[8]

Soon, other organizations appeared, such as the National Association of Colored Women (founded by Harriet Tubman, Frances E. W. Harper, Ida Bell Wells-Barnett, and Mary Church Terrell in 1896). Margaret Murray Washington, wife of African-American activist Booker T. Washington, founded the National Federation of Afro-American Women. Not just interested in women's suffrage, these organizations were active in fighting alcoholism and racism (especially strong in the American South, where lynchings were commonplace). These and many other local organizations brought together tens of thousands of African Americans to fight for equality

United States to vote shall not be denied or abridged by the United States or any State on account of sex." Anthony and others were finally able to persuade Congress to vote on the amendment in 1887, though it was defeated.

Meanwhile, Lucy Stone and the AWSA were working to pressure individual states to legalize women's suffrage, with little success. For the next several years, the NWSA and AWSA worked independently to bring women's suffrage to America. But there was a growing sentiment that if the movement were to succeed, it could only happen if women were united.

In 1890, Elizabeth Cady Stanton turned seventy-five, Susan B. Anthony turned seventy, and Lucy Stone turned seventy-two. Anthony and Cady Stanton felt betrayed by Stone when she left the NWSA in 1869, and the tensions between the women lasted a long time. For the women's suffrage movement to move forward, those old wounds would have to be healed. To bring the two organizations together, Harriot Stanton Blatch (Cady Stanton's daughter), Alice Stone Blackwell (Lucy Stone's daughter), and others organized a convention, to be held in Washington, D.C. In February 1890, the AWSA and NWSA met there to unite the two organizations. At that point, the National American Women's Suffrage Association (NAWSA) was born. In many ways, it was the passing of the reins to a new generation of women's suffrage activists. No one could adequately fill the roles of Anthony, Cady Stanton, and Stone, who had worked tirelessly for decades and had become significant reformers in American history. But the movement was entering a new phase, and young women were needed to finish the work their mothers had begun.

That same year, 1890, the Wyoming Territory, the first territory to legalize women's suffrage, entered the Union with women's suffrage still intact as the forty-fourth state. By 1900, Colorado, Utah, and Idaho also approved women's suffrage. Some states were legalizing women's suffrage, but there was still no federal law giving women the vote. It seemed only a matter of time, but when would that time come?

By 1900, women in four western states were able to cast their votes.

Chapter | 7 |

The Final Push

Lucy Stone died in 1893 at the age of seventy-five; Elizabeth Cady Stanton died at the age of seventy-seven in 1902; and Susan B. Anthony, eighty-six years old, died in 1906. To the sadness and frustration of tens of thousands of suffrage activists, those women died before their dream of women's suffrage would come true. But they had planted a tree that would ultimately bear fruit.

A final push was needed to legalize women's suffrage. But the three great heroes—Cady Stanton, Stone, and Anthony—were gone. Fortunately, there were, at the turn of the twentieth century, tens of thousands of women now committed to the cause. This new generation had the energy and dedication to finish the job.

The Anti-Women's Suffrage Movement

After the Civil War, the cult of domesticity began to lose its strong hold on the American imagination. The "true

Alice Stone Blackwell and Harriot Stanton Blatch

Alice Stone Blackwell

Two important women's suffrage activists who followed Elizabeth Cady Stanton and Lucy Stone were their daughters, Harriot Stanton Blatch and Alice Stone Blackwell. Both were practically born into the women's suffrage movement. They were college graduates and working professionals. Like their mothers, both devoted their entire lives to women's rights. Blatch and Blackwell had remarkably similar careers—they worked to recruit working-class women to the suffrage cause. Blackwell was involved in the Women's Trade Union League, and Blatch was in the Women's Political Union. Both women gained fame as writers. Blackwell was the editor of *The Women's Journal*, and Blatch was one of the cowriters of *The History of Woman Suffrage*. Most important, both were key figures in reinvigorating the women's suffrage movement following the deaths of Anthony, Cady Stanton, and Stone.

Harriot Stanton Blatch

woman" was being replaced by the "new woman." The "true woman" had to stay at home, but the "new woman" now had more opportunities. No longer confined to the home, the "new woman" could seek fulfillment in other arenas. More and more women were becoming doctors, lawyers, and professors. Men had traditionally held these careers.

But not everyone welcomed the "new woman." There were still many people in America who longed for the days when women "knew their place," that is, in the home. Many saw the "new woman" as a threat to the traditional way of life. And, to them, perhaps the biggest threat was women's suffrage. As a result of this fear, many antisuffrage organizations began to appear.

Surprisingly, many women—in addition to men— were involved in the antisuffrage movement. Just three years after the Seneca Falls Convention, in 1851, Mrs. Albert T. Leatherbee of Boston had published *The Anti-Suffrage Campaign Manual*. In it, she argued that women's suffrage "will not be a progressive step, but a retrogressive one."[1] In 1872, one thousand people signed a petition to the U.S. Congress to deny the vote to women. Two of the most high-profile signers of that petition were wives of famous Civil War officers: Eleanor Sherman, wife of General William Sherman, and Madeleine Dahlgren, wife of Admiral John Dahlgren.[2] Afterward, antisuffrage organizations began to appear,

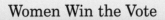

including the Massachusetts Anti-Suffrage Committee, the National Association Opposed to Woman Suffrage, and the Women's National Anti-Suffrage League. There was even an antisuffrage newspaper, *The Remonstrance*, which operated from 1890 to 1908.

Many historians note that most women who opposed women's suffrage were wealthy and feared that women's suffrage would threaten their privileged position in society. But there were other factors as well. The southern states were afraid that giving the vote to black women, in addition to black men (the Fifteenth Amendment), would threaten Southern white supremacy. In addition, American alcohol interests feared that, because so many American women were involved in temperance organizations, granting women's suffrage might result in a ban on alcoholic drinks. This threat against alcohol interests ensured that anti-women's suffrage organizations were very well financed. The alcohol businesses spared no expense in fighting women's suffrage.[3] According to Eileen L. McDonagh and H. Douglas Price, "The presumed alliance between the woman suffrage movement and the prohibition movement cost the suffrage movement dearly, as the suffrage cause automatically inherited the enemies of prohibition, most notably, the brewing interests."[4]

But perhaps the most powerful opponent of women's suffrage after the turn of the twentieth century was Woodrow Wilson, the twenty-eighth president of the United States. By the time he became president in 1913, the women's suffrage movement had made great strides toward earning women the vote, but Wilson fiercely opposed women's suffrage. He was "the principle antagonist in the final chapter of the long battle for suffrage."[5] Would anyone be able to challenge such a powerful man? Fortunately for the women's suffrage cause, one woman who rose to the challenge was Alice Paul.

A New Voice for the Right to Vote

Alice Paul was born in 1885 in New Jersey, and, like women's rights pioneers Lucretia Mott and Susan B. Anthony, Paul was a Quaker. However, unlike Anthony and Mott, Paul was born at a time when there were far more educational and professional opportunities available to women. Of course, those new opportunities were due in large part to the work of Mott and Anthony. Paul was the oldest of four children born to William and Tacie Paul. William Paul was a successful banker who supported Alice in her educational ambitions. Alice went to a Quaker school as a child and then to Swarthmore College, where she majored in biology. A brilliant student, Alice Paul continued her education after Swarthmore, ultimately earning a doctorate in sociology from the University of Pennsylvania. She also studied

This image of Alice Paul was originally printed in a publication called *The Suffragist* on December 25, 1915.

economics and politics in England and earned a law degree from American University in Washington, D.C. She was, during her lifetime, one of the most educated women in history.

It was during her studies in England that Paul became a women's suffrage advocate. Walking along London streets in 1907, Paul stumbled on a small crowd gathered around a woman arguing for British women's suffrage. That woman was Christabel Pankhurst, daughter of the most famous women's suffrage activist in England, Emmeline Pankhurst.

Paul befriended the Pankhursts and joined the

Emmeline Pankhurst

A major influence on the final push toward American women's suffrage was Englishwoman Emmeline Pankhurst. Together with her two daughters, Christabel and Sylvia, Pankhurst organized the Women's Social and Political Union (WSPU) in 1903 to promote women's suffrage in England. When the British government ignored the WSPU's polite efforts to gain the vote, the organization resorted to more radical methods. WSPU members staged street rallies, broke into government meetings, and committed many acts of civil disobedience, including hunger strikes, to gain publicity for women's suffrage. Between 1907 and 1914, Emmeline Pankhurst was arrested many times, often enduring beatings and force-feedings. England granted women the right to vote

Women's Social and Political Union (WSPU), the organization fighting for women's suffrage in England. On two occasions, Paul was arrested and jailed while participating in women's suffrage protests. During her second imprisonment, a thirty-day jail sentence, Paul refused to eat—a strategy known as a "hunger strike"—in order to call attention to women's suffrage. She also wanted to shame the police into releasing her early. She was not released early, however. Instead, she was "force-fed," a painful process in which a tube was stuck down her throat to give her liquid food. When the twenty-five-year-old Paul returned to the United States in 1910, she was in poor health from her grueling experience in England. But she was ready to fight for women's suffrage in the same way that Pankhurst was fighting in England. After completing her doctoral studies in 1912, Paul joined the National American Women's Suffrage Association (NAWSA).

The women's suffrage movement needed Paul's energy. Since the deaths of Anthony, Cady Stanton, and Stone, the movement had stalled, entering a phase historians today call "the doldrums."[6] The president of the NAWSA since 1904 had been Dr. Anna Howard Shaw. American suffragists greatly admired Shaw, a powerful public speaker. However, she was making little headway toward gaining a constitutional suffrage amendment. The NAWSA put Paul in charge of the Congressional

Committee, whose job was to fight for a constitutional amendment. Paul knew that what was needed was a big splash.

Toward Success

That splash came on March 3, 1913, the day before Woodrow Wilson was inaugurated as president. Bringing together thousands of people dedicated to women's suffrage, Paul organized the Women's Suffrage Parade. Starting at the Capitol building, eight thousand marchers made their way up Pennsylvania Avenue, passing the White House, and ending at the Hall of the Daughters of the American Revolution. At the head of the parade, sitting boldly atop a white horse, was Inez Milholland Boissevain, who carried a purple, white, and gold banner. The banner colors were "purple for the royal glory of women, white for purity at home and in politics, gold for the crown of the victor."[7]

Soon after the parade began, however, things turned ugly. Men in the crowd hurled insults at the women, telling them to go back home where they belonged. The hecklers also targeted the men who marched with the women, shouting, "henpecko" and "Where are your skirts?"[8] Soon the mob was hurling objects at the marchers, blocking their pathway and finally attacking them. Though police were there to keep order, they did nothing as the marchers were assaulted. The attackers

The official program for the women's suffrage procession in Washington, D.C., on March 13, 1913, shows a woman on horseback at the head of the procession. From the woman's long horn, a "Votes for Women" banner blows in the wind. The U.S. Capitol is in background.

injured hundreds of marchers. There was a massive public outcry because of the violence. The tide was turning in the suffragists' favor. But Wilson, who was to become president the next day, was unmoved.

Not everyone in the NAWSA was happy with Paul's energetic style. The president of the NAWSA, Dr. Anna Howard Shaw, believed that the quickest path to gaining nationwide suffrage was to petition the individual states. (This had been Lucy Stone's strategy, too.) But between 1869 and 1913, only nine states had adopted women's suffrage, all of them western states far from the nation's capital. The new generation of suffragists, led by Paul, did not want to wait for state-by-state suffrage, a process that might take decades, especially in the American South. The new generation of suffragists wanted a constitutional amendment now. But unfortunately, in early 1914, Shaw and her supporters expelled Paul from the NAWSA.

Undaunted, Paul organized her own suffrage organization, the Congressional Union (CU). The CU traveled the nation, recruiting men and women to the cause. Based on her aggressive efforts, Paul managed to convince the U.S. House of Representatives to vote on a suffrage amendment in 1914. The vote failed, 204-174, but the closeness of the vote gave women hope that a constitutional amendment would eventually pass.

President Woodrow Wilson had a change in heart by 1916. Though he had been strongly against women's

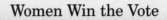

suffrage during his first term, he gradually began to warm to the idea. While campaigning for a second four-year presidential term, President Wilson told an audience that he supported a suffrage amendment: "We feel the tide; we rejoice in the strength of it, and we shall not quarrel in the long run as to the method of it."[9] Soon the suffragists' time would come.

Wilson won reelection in November 1916, and the suffragists were convinced that the president was now on their side. But when Congress did not immediately

Women used banners like this when they marched in support of women's suffrage. The slogan of the movement "Votes for Women" is printed on the banner.

pass a suffrage amendment, the suffragists took to the picket lines again. In early 1917, Paul's CU members stood outside the White House gates, many holding signs that read "Mr. President, What Will You Do For Woman's Suffrage?" and "How Long Must Women Wait For Liberty?"[10] Though President Wilson by then had formally announced his support of women's suffrage, no congressional vote would occur until early 1918. On

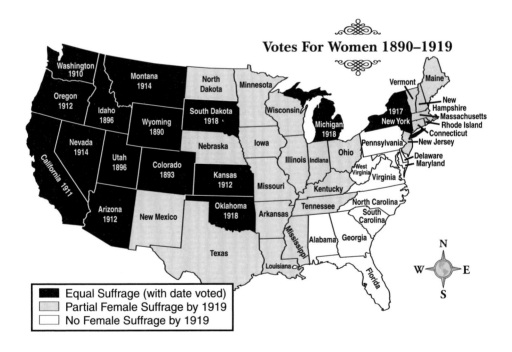

Votes For Women 1890–1919

Equal Suffrage (with date voted)
Partial Female Suffrage by 1919
No Female Suffrage by 1919

This map shows the places that allowed women to vote before the states ratified the Nineteenth Amendment.

January 10, 1918, the House of Representatives voted on the "Susan B. Anthony Amendment," that is, an amendment granting women the right to vote. And, finally, the amendment passed 274 to 136. But the passage of the "Anthony Amendment" in the House of Representatives did not grant women the right to vote. It would still have to pass in the U.S. Senate in order for it to become law. It was a slow process, and women would have to wait a year and a half for the Senate to pass the amendment.

The problem was that in order for a constitutional amendment to pass, it had to receive a two-thirds majority in the Senate. On its first vote in January 1918, the amendment passed 62–34. It was a majority, but it was two votes short of the mandatory two-thirds majority. Suffrage would have to wait another year.

In 1919, the two-thirds majority necessary to pass a constitutional amendment in Congress had been achieved. Though Congress was filled primarily with men, generations of women's suffrage activism had managed to convince most of them that women had now earned the right to vote. On June 4, 1919, Congress officially approved the "Anthony Amendment," 56 votes for and 25 votes against.

The next step was ratification. Three-fourths of the state legislatures had to approve, or ratify, the amendment. The Nineteenth Amendment to the United States

Constitution was officially ratified on August 18, 1920. Entering the U. S. Constitution would be the following law: "The right of citizens of the United States to vote shall not be denied or abridged by the United States or by any State on account of sex." Thanks to the pioneering work of thousands of women's rights advocates during almost two centuries, American women now had the right to vote.

Alice Paul hangs a banner from the balcony of the National Woman's Party headquarters in celebration of the ratification of the Nineteenth Amendment.

Chapter 8

The Legacy of Women's Suffrage

The story of women's suffrage in America is a story of courage, tragedy, heartbreak, patience, and finally triumph. The nineteenth-century suffrage pioneers fought for voting rights against seemingly insurmountable odds. Lucy Stone, the founder of the American Women's Suffrage Association, saved pennies and nickels for nine years before she was able to go to Oberlin College. Sojourner Truth, a former slave, cleaned white people's homes in order to make enough money to give her famous speeches. Many had to struggle against their own communities and their own families in order to "get the vote."

In 1869, when Wyoming became the first territory to grant suffrage to women, it seemed that nationwide women's suffrage was just around the corner. But American women had to wait fifty more years for a constitutional women's suffrage amendment. The three most famous suffragists—Lucy Stone, Susan B. Anthony, and

Although Susan B. Anthony (left) and Elizabeth Cady Stanton did not live to see the passage of the Nineteenth Amendment, it was through their great efforts that women are able to vote today.

Elizabeth Cady Stanton—worked tirelessly for decades to win women's suffrage. But none of them would live long enough to cast a vote in a national election. Despite that fact, by the time of those women's deaths in the first decade of the twentieth century, tens of thousands of women and men were dedicated to the cause. Those new activists inherited the bravery and work ethic of those three great pioneers, qualities they would certainly need in the final push toward victory for women's suffrage.

Tradition, special interests (such as antisuffrage organizations and alcoholic beverage companies), and prejudice were united against women's suffrage. But the new generation, who now had education and employment advantages that their mothers never had, was ready for the fight. When victory was finally won in 1920, those voting women knew that their right to vote had been earned by the labors of many generations of suffrage activists.

When American women were granted suffrage in 1920, their work was far from over. In the same way that nineteenth-century suffragists were often abolitionists as well, many twentieth-century suffragists were also committed to other causes. So when they won the vote, they did not stop working. When the Nineteenth Amendment was ratified in 1920, there were only eleven countries in the world where women could vote.[1] After winning their own vote, many American suffragists

Less than one hundred years after women won the right to vote, Senator Hillary Rodham Clinton came very close to earning the Democratic Party's nomination for president. Below, Clinton speaks during a campaign rally at Indiana University in Bloomington on April 25, 2008.

turned their attention to international women's suffrage. Alice Paul said, "Women are the same the world over, no matter what country they live in. They want a worldwide movement, like a church, something universal."[2] Paul and thousands like her worked to bring voting rights to women all over the world. But it was not just voting rights they were interested in. They were concerned with larger issues of equality. Suffrage was just one of many issues facing modern women.

For centuries, women were under the strict control of men. Women were excluded from education, most forms of employment, government, and legal rights. Furthermore, that exclusion existed all over the world. So when women gained the right to vote, they knew that, in many ways, their fight had just begun. Like men, they too wanted to live in a world in which they could have the freedom to be whatever they wanted to be. In 1776, John Adams famously told his wife, Abigail, that the Declaration of Independence pertained only to men. "All men are created equal," he reminded her. But Abigail Adams, Olympe de Gouges, and Mary Wollstonecraft knew then what women today know: Given the chance, they could prove that all people are created equal.

TIMELINE

1776—Declaration of Independence; Abigail Adams writes to husband, John Adams, to "remember the ladies."

1789—French Revolution begins; *Declaration of the Rights of Man* published; U.S. Constitution ratified; Women's March to Versailles.

1790—Lucretia Mott born in Nantucket, Massachusetts; Mary Wollstonecraft writes *A Vindication of the Rights of Woman.*

1791—Olympe de Gouges writes *Declaration of the Rights of Woman.*

1815—Elizabeth Cady Stanton born in Johnstown, New York.

1818—Lucy Stone born near West Brookfield, Massachusetts.

1820—Susan B. Anthony born in Adams, Massachusetts.

1821—Troy Female Seminary opens.

1837—Oberlin College becomes first college in the United States to admit women; Mount Holyoke Female Seminary opens as the first American college for women only.

1840—Women denied participation at World Anti-Slavery Convention in London.

1848—Seneca Falls Convention held.

1850—First National Women's Rights Convention held in Worcester, Massachusetts.

1866—Susan B. Anthony, Lucy Stone, Elizabeth Cady Stanton, and Frederick Douglass organize the American Equal Rights Association (AERA).

1869—Susan B. Anthony and Elizabeth Cady Stanton organize the National Woman Suffrage Association (NWSA); Women granted suffrage in Wyoming Territory.

1870—Lucy Stone leaves the NWSA and forms the American Woman Suffrage Asociation (AWSA); Fifteenth Amendment, granting suffrage to African American men, is ratified.

1872—Susan B. Anthony is arrested while attempting to vote in presidential election.

1890—The NWSA and AWSA unite to form the National American Woman Suffrage Association (NAWSA).

1893—Lucy Stone dies at age seventy-five.

1902—Elizabeth Cady Stanton dies at age seventy-seven.

1906—Susan B. Anthony dies at age eighty-six

1915—Women's suffrage bill loses by vote of 204-174 in U.S. House of Representatives.

1919— U.S. Senate passes women's suffrage bill by vote of 56-25.

1920—Nineteenth Amendment to U.S. Constitution is ratified, granting women the right to vote.

CHAPTER NOTES

Chapter 1. Victory in Wyoming

1. T. A. Larson, *History of Wyoming, 2nd edition* (Lincoln: University of Nebraska Press, 1978), p. 71.

2. Dorothy Gray, *Women of the West* (Lincoln: University of Nebraska Press, 1998), p. 77.

3. Larson, p. 83.

4. Marcy Lynn Karin, "Esther Morris and Her Equality State: From Council Bill 70 to Life on the Bench," *The American Journal of Legal History*, Volume 46, 2004, p. 320.

5. Ibid., p. 333.

6. Ibid., p. 336.

Chapter 2. A New Country

1. Marchette Chute, *The First Liberty: A History of the Right to Vote In America*, 1619–1850 (New York: Dutton, 1969), p. 196.

2. Elizabeth Cady Stanton, Susan B. Anthony, Matilda Joslyn Gage, and Ida Husted Harper, ed., *History of Woman Suffrage,* vol. 1 (New York: Arno, 1969), p. 32.

3. *Thomas Paine, Common Sense* (New York: Wiley, 1942), p. 53.

Chapter 3. England and Early America

1. Mary Wollstonecraft, *A Vindication of the Rights of Woman*, Norton Critical Edition, Ed. Carol H. Poston (New York: Norton, 1988), p. 9.

2. Ibid., p. 12.

3. Ibid., p. 147.

4. Ibid., p. 242.

5. Martha J. Cutter, "Beyond Stereotypes: Mary Wilkins Freeman's Radical Critique of Nineteenth-Century Cults of Femininity," *Women's Studies*, Vol. 21, 1992, p. 384.

6. Ibid.

7. XX De la Banta, *De la Banta's Advice to Ladies Concerning Beauty* (Chicago: S. Junkin, 1878), p. 288, qtd. in *American Women: A Gateway to Library of Congress Resources for the Study of Women's History and Culture in the United States*, n.d., < http://memory.loc.gov/ ammem/awhhtml/awgc1/etiquette.html> (March 20, 2008).

8. "Biographical Overview," *Emma Willard School*, n.d., <http:// www.emmawillard.org/about/history/ehwillard/ehwillard.php> (March 18, 2008).

9. Elisabeth Griffith, *In Her Own Right: The Life of Elizabeth Cady Stanton* (New York: Oxford University Press, 1984), p. 18.

10. "Biographical Overview."

11. Sally Schwager, "Educating Women in America," *Signs*, Volume 12.2, 1987, p. 343.

Chapter 4. The Seneca Falls Convention

1. Alison M. Parker, "The Case for Reform Antecedents," *Votes for Women: The Struggle for Suffrage Revisited*, Ed. Jean Baker (New York: Oxford University Press, 2002), p. 23.

2. Elizabeth Cady Stanton, Susan B. Anthony, Matilda Joslyn Gage, and Ida Husted Harper, ed., *History of Woman Suffrage,* vol. 1 (New York: Arno, 1969), p. 88.

3. Elizabeth Cady Stanton, *Elizabeth Cady Stanton, As Revealed in Her Letters, Diary, and Reminiscences, Vol.* 1, Eds. Theodore Stanton and Harriot Stanton Blatch (New York: Harper & Row, 1922), p. 79.

4. Frederick Douglass, "Why I Became a Woman's Rights Man," Audio Recording, Victory Audio Video Services, 1995.

5. Stanton, p. 140.

6. Otelia Cromwell, *Lucretia Mott* (Cambridge: Harvard University Press, 1958), p. 93.

7. Stanton, p. 145.

8. *Woman Suffrage*, vol. 1, p. 67.

9. Elisabeth Griffith, *In Her Own Right: The Life of Elizabeth Cady Stanton* (New York: Oxford University Press, 1984), p. 55.

10. Cady Stanton refers to him only as "an embryo professor of Yale College" (*Woman Suffrage,* Vol. 1, p. 69).

11. Griffith, p. 57.

Chapter 5. More Women Seek the Vote

1. Kathleen Barry, *Susan B. Anthony: A Biography of a Singular Feminist* (New York: New York University Press, 1988), p. 23.

2. Ibid., p. 25.

3. Elizabeth Cady Stanton, Susan B. Anthony, Matilda Joslyn Gage, and Ida Husted Harper, ed., *History of Woman Suffrage,* vol. 1 (New York: Arno, 1969), p. 457.

4. Ida Husted Harper, *The Life and Work of Susan B. Anthony: Including Public Addresses, Her Own Letters and Many from Her Contemporaries During Fifty Years, Vol. 1* (New York: Arno, 1969), p. 64.

5. Perhaps the most infamous incidence of the Fugitive Slave Law involved the seizure of Anthony Burns. Burns was a former slave who had escaped to the North. Burns became a well-respected minister in Boston. Slave hunters arrested him in Boston on May 24, 1854 and returned him to his "owner," Charles F. Suttle in Virginia. Suttle sold Burns to a North Carolina slave owner named David McDaniel. In 1856, McDaniel then sold Burns to the abolitionist Leonard Grimes. A free man, Burns returned to Boston. He died in Canada on July 17, 1862. For further study, see Charles Emery Stevens, *Anthony Burns: A History* (Boston: Jewett and Company, 1856).

6. Rosalyn Terborg-Penn, *African American Women in the Struggle for the Vote, 1850–1920* (Bloomington: Indiana University Press, 1998).

7. Richard O. Reisem, "Rochester Remembers the Civil War With Cannon, Sculpture, and 399 Tombstones," *Epitaph Newsletter*, Volume 18.2, 1998, <http://www.lib.rochester.edu/ index.cfm?PAGE= 3098> (June 25, 2007).

Chapter 6. Battles Lost and Won

1. Ida Husted Harper, *The Life and Work of Susan B. Anthony: Including Public Addresses, Her Own Letters and Many from Her Contemporaries During Fifty Years, Vol. 1* (New York: Arno, 1969), 323.

2. Ibid., p. 324.

3. "Amendment XIV," *Legal Information Institute*, n.d., <http://www.law.cornell.edu/constitution/constitution.amendmentxiv.html> (March 7, 2008).

4. Elizabeth Cady Stanton, Susan B. Anthony, Matilda Joslyn Gage, and Ida Husted Harper, ed., *History of Woman Suffrage,* vol. 2 (New York: Arno, 1969), p. 757.

5. Kathleen Barry, *Susan B. Anthony: A Biography of a Singular Feminist* (New York: New York University Press, 1988), p. 250.

6. *The New York Times*, November 29, 1872, p. 1.

7. *The Times*, July 4, 1873, p. C5.

8. Rosalyn Terborg-Penn, *African American Women in the Struggle for the Vote*, 1850–1920 (Bloomington: Indiana University Press, 1998), p. 83.

Chapter 7. The Final Push

1. "Editorial," *Women's Studies*, Volume 1, 1973, p. 245.

2. Eleanor Flexner, *Century of Struggle: The Woman's Rights Movement in the United States* (Cambridge, Mass.: Belknap, 1959), p. 295.

3. Ibid, pp. 294–305.

4. Eileen L. McDonagh and H. Douglas Price, "Woman Suffrage in the Progressive Era: Patterns of Opposition and Support in Referenda Voting, 1910–1918" *The American Political Science Review*, Volume 79.2, 1985, p. 419.

5. Eleanor Clift, *Founding Sisters and the Nineteenth Amendment* (Hoboken, N.J.: John Wiley & Sons, 2003), p. 91.

6. Flexner, p. 248

7. Clift, p. 91.

8. Ibid., p. 92.

9. Flexner, p. 279.

10. Ibid., p. 282.

Chapter 8. The Legacy of Women's Suffrage

1. New Zealand (1893), Australia (1902), Norway (1913), Denmark (1915), Canada (1917), Austria (1918), Germany (1918), Poland (1918), Russia (1918), The Netherlands (1919), and the United States (1920).

2. Jean Baker, *Sisters: The Lives of America's Suffragists* (New York: Hill and Wang, 2005), p. 228.

GLOSSARY

abolition—The banning of slavery.

amendment—A change to the U.S. Constitution.

antisuffrage—Believing that women should not have the right to vote.

Congress—The lawmaking body of government in the United States, which includes the Senate and the House of Representatives.

Constitution—The original document outlining the laws of the United States.

cult of domesticity—The belief that women should not work outside the home.

federalism—A theory that supports sharing power between the federal government and the states.

manumission—Freedom from slavery.

misogyny—The hatred of women.

Prohibition—A ban on the sale of alcoholic drinks in the United States.

ratify—To approve.

suffrage—The right to vote.

veto—To deny.

FURTHER READING

Bausum, Ann. *With Courage and Cloth: Winning the Fight for a Woman's Right to Vote.* Washington, D.C.: National Geographic, 2004.

Bozonelis, Helen Koutras. *A Look at the Nineteenth Amendment: Women Win the Right to Vote.* Berkeley Heights, N.J.: Enslow Publishers, Inc., 2008.

Burgan, Michael. *Elizabeth Cady Stanton: Social Reformer.* Minneapolis: Compass Point Books, 2006.

——*The 19th Amendment.* Minneapolis: Compass Point Books, 2006.

Connolly, Sean. *Right to Vote.* North Mankato, Minn.: Smart Apple Media, 2006.

Donlan, Leni. *Working for Change: The Struggle for Women's Right to Vote.* Chicago: Raintree, 2008.

Frost-Knappman, Elizabeth, and Kathryn Cullen DuPont. *Women's Suffrage in America.* New York: Facts on File, 2005.

McPherson, Stephanie Sammartino. *Susan B. Anthony.* Minneapolis: Learner Publications, Co., 2006.

Mountjoy, Shane. *The Women's Rights Movement: Moving Toward Equality.* New York: Chelsea House Pub., 2008.

Rau, Dana Meachen. *Great Women of the Suffrage Movement.* Minneapolis: Compass Point Books, 2006.

Internet Addresses

The Library of Congress: One Hundred Years Toward
Suffrage: An Overview

**<http://memory.loc.gov/ammem/vfwhtml/
vfwtl.html>**

A detailed timeline of the women's suffrage movement.

PBS Kids Go! Women and the Vote: Alice Paul's Fight
for Suffrage

**<http://pbskids.org/wayback/civilrights/
features_suffrage.html>**

Describes one woman's fight to win the vote.

The Susan B. Anthony Center for Women's Leadership:
Suffrage History

**<http://www.rochester.edu/sba/
suffragehistory.html>**

*This site has a lot of links to various aspects of
suffrage history.*

Index